The Leadership Shift:

The Strategic Positioning of Latino Business Leaders

Published by Aspire 4 Life, Inc., New York, New York.

Library of Congress Cataloging-in-Publication Data is available.
  Dr. Nilda Perez. The Leadership Shift: The Strategic Positioning of Latino Business Leaders.

ISBN-13: 978-0615947457

    1. Latino Americans – Emotional Intelligence, Drivers of Change, leadership shift, Latinos in business leadership

Cover Design by: Alessandro I Calderon, Jr.

Published in the United States by Aspire 4 Life, Inc.

The Leadership Shift:

The Strategic Positioning of Latino Business Leaders

Dr. Nilda Perez

New York: NY

DEDICATION

I dedicate this book to my family who has supported me through these last 3.5 years while I was creating my dream. Thank you, Esther, Mom, Andrew, and AJ for your time, patience, love and support. And I want to thank Ken Lord for his assistance in bringing it all together.

Table of Contents

FOREWORD

I learned about leadership early. It was inevitable. My father, Rafael, was a naval officer and our family was brought up on "doing a good job," respect, the importance of character, and ethical behavior. Rafael retired from the US Navy as a Rear Admiral and went on to be assistant Dean of the Law School at the University of Miami.

Leadership was woven into our lives and, I as the oldest of three, naturally assumed the leadership role. Leadership is important to me. It is a subject I've written about in a book, *Latinization and the Latino Leader,* with my co-author, Marlene Gonzalez. I teach a course on it at DePaul University. But, why is this important? I've witnessed the growth of the Latino population since the 80's and worked with major corporations marketing and selling to this valuable consumer. It only seemed a matter of time when these same corporations would be looking to hire professionals has part of a complete Latino effort.

The Leadership Shift: The Strategic Positioning of Latino Business Leaders time has come. "The one thing that distinguishes Latinos is their innate ability to work hard, be dependable, show loyalty and have integrity," states Dr. Perez. These are the very Latino innate qualities she identifies that create the leadership shift. It is time for Latino leaders to emerge and we see this happening in politics, education, science, the arts and more. What Dr. Perez does in this well—written book, is provide concrete reasons why this shift is happening.

With a focus on scholarly research she creates a well—substantiated argument for the rise of the Latino leader. Beginning with Latino's historical framework, and moving into an analysis of emotional intelligence, cultural intelligence, values and core beliefs, Dr. Perez creates a blueprint for an aspiring Latino leader. As a business coach her thoughtful analysis of strategic foresight creates scenarios that encourage the rise of the servant leader. Latinos possess natural qualities of collectivism, family oriented values and caring about the welfare of their community.

Moving further into the shift, our globalized world is today's community. Latinos are comfortable in this world because of their own intercultural experiences. Each of their countries of origin is rich in diversity – indigenous, Spanish, mestizo. This ease with people from different viewpoints provides employers an extra layer of cultural intelligence (CQ) that will only benefit the future of business.

Yet another layer of the shift is the growth of Latino business and rise of the Latino upscale and middle class. A study by the Association of Hispanic Advertising Agencies (AHAA) in 2012 projects this segment to grow to 35 million by 2050. These higher incomes fuel education levels resulting in increased graduation and attainment of graduate degrees.

Dr. Perez closes her book using a spiritual lens that guides her life. Using biblical references and examples, she paints scenarios with carefully constructed guides for the Latino leader and the general reader.

This is a book to read, and use as a guide to develop and promote Latino leaders. It is template for companies looking to hire them. It has a place on the bookshelf or kindle that will inspire and promote *The Leadership Shift: The Strategic Positioning of Latino Business Leaders*.

Cristina Benitez

Director Latino Media & Communication
DePaul University, Chicago
Latinization – How Latino Culture Is Transforming the US, Author
Latinization and Latino Leadership, Co-authors, Cristina Benitez & Marlene Gonzalez

Preface

This book was developed from research I did for my doctoral work at Regent University. I am thankful for great chairman Dr. Bramwell Osula, and professors Dr. Gary Oster, Dr. Jay Gary, and Dr. Doris Gomez who encouraged me to pursue my dream and find the answers to pressing questions.

I had for some time been intrigued by the fact that there has always been a scarcity in Latino leaders in the U.S. Also, Latino businesses, I found, were few and far between and even then most remained small business for their lifetime of the business. My father owned several businesses and this was my first exposure to small business and my awareness of other Latino business owners.

My research led to some poignant information which started me on a journey to explore questions such as: how Latinos came to the U.S. from the onset, what has kept many from significant professional growth, what qualities Latinos have that can pave the way for leadership roles, and how can they establish themselves as successful business leaders. The findings were fascinating. And as the information unfolded, I found such great hope for the establishment of successful Latino business leaders.

In my search for what qualifies Latinos to become successful business leaders I found a trend that is consistently shifting leadership roles to Latinos. The Latino is inherently global, a quality that is imperative to today's business leader. The instinctive qualities that the Latino possesses will make the Latino the most logical choice for leadership roles in the very near future. Latinos have been gaining ground as they see the need for their competencies. This book will highlight the relevance of the Latino as leader. This book was born as a result of this fascinating information.

Introduction

The Leadership Shift: The Positioning of Latino Business Leaders

The Latino Leadership Shift: *The Positioning of Latino Leaders* is a six-part series which began as a dissertation and unfolded into this book and a series of presentations. It was created from the understanding that currently there is transference of leadership and Latinos are at the forefront of assuming leadership roles. These chapters build sequentially, bringing you, the reader, on a journey from the early history of the Latino in the U.S. to a in-depth understanding of who the Latino is, what qualifies the Latino for business leadership, and how to watch for the trends and strategically strengthen your abilities. The intention of this book is to set the framework for understanding what you, the Latino/a, bring to the leadership role and to enforce the urgency to develop skills for this shift.

Six areas will be addressed in this book:

➢1) the growth in the Latino population

➢2) the increase in Latino business owners

➢3) how the Latino is ripe for leadership

➢4) what qualifies Latinos for leadership

➢5) what the Latino has to contribute to leadership

➤6) why Latinos are presently the most logical choice for leadership.

The time is now; Latinos need be prepared for this inevitable shift in leadership and position themselves to lead. Throughout this book you will find that we will use both the word 'Latino' and 'Hispanic;' at the core they mean the same thing: an individual from Latin American descent. In the world they are known as Latino or Latino Americano. In the U.S., the word is "Hispanic." Both describe the descent of Spanish speaking origin.

Chapter 1

Leadership: The Latino Influence in the U.S.

We begin with a structure that describes who Latinos are, how they got to the U.S., and how the trends are positioning Latinos for leadership . In this framework, a foundation is built that identifies Latino/Hispanic history, their present state, and their future. In this chapter, our timeline is divided into three parts:

➢ Hindsight—a review of the history of Hispanics in the U.S.

➢ Insight—illustrating the trends that have changed the Latino population in notable ways such as immigrant status, median age, health, societal prototype, education and economic status, and the shift that has made Latinos a most desirable commodity, and lastly;

➢ Foresight—how these current trends position Latinos to lead in the future.

> *"Remember, remember always that all of U.S., and you and I especially, are descended from immigrants..."*
>
> *Franklin D. Roosevelt*

Did This Shift Happen Suddenly?

To everyone's surprise, the 2000 U.S. census discovered that the Latino population was growing exponentially. This discovery not only surprised many Americans, but it also became a cause for concern—especially to the Caucasian population. Then the 2010 U.S. Census reported another dramatic increase of forty-three percent in the Latino population from 2000. The forecast purports that the Latino population will grow minimally to ninety-plus million by 2050. The United States is on a path to ethnic plurality (U.S. Census). This is an unprecedented paradigm shift. The country's vibrant demographic compositions, and its healthy multicultural dynamic, are critical assets to the U.S. in global economic competition. Latinos are at the heart of this asset. They will be for some considerable future. According to Glenn Llopis, Hispanics will actually save American corporations (Llopis, 2012).

> *"The way Americans most understand the history of Latinos in this country, a lot of it is being told now through the lens of what's happening with the immigration debate. While that's an important debate that has security and moral implications, in my view, there's also a huge history of Latinos in the United States that's never been told.*
>
> *Ken Salazar*

Hindsight: Where did all these Latinos come from?

Latinos: Old and New

More than any other ethnic group, Hispanics are at once both a new and a traditional population composed of both newcomers and old timers who have deep roots in the American soil. Hispanics comprise a population that can allege both a history and a territory in what is today the United States; this precedes the establishment of the nation. Concurrently, the Hispanic population *appears* to have emerged suddenly and is growth-driven by an accelerating emigration from the Spanish-speaking countries of Latin America (The National Research Council). Many of our forbears came to this country to seek a new or better life, fully aware that the cost might be great personal suffering and risk. They migrated to an unfamiliar world leaving loved ones, a familiar land, and culture, to journey into an unknown land with peculiar customs, culture, and language (Abalos, 2007). While simultaneously many Latinos have been in the U.S. almost as long as or longer than many Anglos.

A standard misconception has been that all Latinos are Mexican. Although Mexicans are the largest Latino population (63%), not all Latinos are Mexican. Puerto Ricans are 9.2 percent, Cuban 3.5 percent, Dominican 2.8 percent, and South American 5.5 percent (U.S. Census 2010). History tells the story of where this large population of Latinos originated. On February 2, 1848, the Treaty of Guadalupe Hidalgo was signed. According to the treaty, Mexico ceded to the United States nearly all the territory now included in the states of New Mexico, Utah, Nevada, Arizona, California, Texas, and western Colorado was originally Mexican soil. After the war was won by America, all these states were purchased from Mexico for $15 Million and the U.S. assumption of its citizens claims against Mexico (Britannica.com). Suddenly Mexican's were immigrants in their own land.

This piece of history attests to the extreme numbers of Latinos, namely Mexicans, in the U.S. California and Texas together have the largest number of Mexicans in the entire nation. Latinos are shaped, in part, by the historical and political relationship of Spain with Latin America. They are a racially diverse mix with Spain, and with African and Latin American countries. Yet for Latinos, there is no racial divide. Latinos see themselves solely through language and culture (Cartagena, 2013).

The stereotype is that Latinos are and have always been illegal immigrants, unacculturated, unassimilated (Orozco & Páez, 2002), indigenous, poor, and undereducated (Chavez, 1991). The perception is that Latinos come the U.S. to seek menial jobs, e.g., agriculture and au pair (Chavez). Latinos have been known to be of low socioeconomic status with median household income of $39,005 (Pew Research Center, 2013). Most have been considered undereducated blue collar workers (Gonzlez & Benitez, 2010)

The second largest population of Latinos in the U.S. is the Puerto Ricans. They are also the only Latin Americans who are not immigrants. In 1917, the Jones Act was signed, which established Puerto Ricans as American citizens. There is interdependence between U.S. and Puerto Rico that has a long and complex history. Its political identity is paradoxical and complicated. According to the Pew Research: Hispanic Trends Project an estimated 4.7 million Puerto Ricans reside in the U.S.; this number is slightly greater than the population in Puerto Rico itself, which is currently about 3.7 million. Only one third (1.4 million) of Puerto Rican population was actually born in Puerto Rico. Most Puerto Ricans in the U.S. identify themselves as Puerto Rican descendents. Puerto Ricans born in the island are deemed natives and citizens of the U.S. by birth. Those of Puerto Rican descent born outside of the U.S. or Puerto Rico are not considered U.S. citizens by birth; this is a very small number of people. The regional dispersion of Puerto Rican is concentrated in the Northeast – 52 percent, and then mostly in New York – 23 percent, and now in the South – 30 percent, and most are located in Florida – 18 percent (Motel & Patten).

Another fact about Puerto Ricans, according to Pew Research, is that 82 percent of Puerto Ricans born ages 5 and older are proficient in English language. The other 18 percent are not very proficient compared to 35% of all Latinos. Just as most Latino population in the U.S., the median age of Puerto Ricans is 27 years. Puerto Ricans are less likely than most

Hispanics to be married – 36 percent versus 44 percent of Hispanics in the U.S., which leads to the fact that 64 percent of Puerto women ages 15 to 44 who gave birth were unwed mothers. This rate is significantly higher at 45 percent greater than other Latinas and the U.S. Puerto Ricans have higher levels of education than the overall Hispanic population. Puerto Ricans 25 and older have obtained at least a bachelor's degree at 16 percent higher rate than the 13 percent of all U.S. Hispanics (Motel & Paten). Because Puerto Ricans are U.S. citizens, whether they are native born or U.S. born, they are afforded more opportunities than foreign born Hispanics.

Religion and Culture

Historically and culturally, most Latinos have been Catholic; even if not Catholic, they have a strong belief in God and often in Christianity (Abalos, 2007). Unlike most immigrants, Latinos have refused to discard their language, culture, music, and food (Bedolla, 2005). Latinos are proud of their heritage (Cartagena) and many, especially the second and third generations, consider themselves to be 100% Latino as well as 100% American (Abalos). Because many Latinos have lived between two worlds they move with ease from one to the other, frequently living in both. Latinos are multilingual, speaking Spanish, English and "Spanglish." Language is extremely important to Latinos; not speaking Spanish is frowned upon.

Individuals of Latin American descent are identified under the categories Spanish (because of the language) or

"Hispanic"—a term created in 1970 by the U.S. Census to identify people of Spanish speaking origin (U.S. Census) or Latino/a. These terms that will be used interchangeably throughout this presentation. These are the roots of the Latino-American.

Insight: Understanding the Trend

The Change in the Types of Hispanic Immigrant

According to the Pew Hispanic Center, the number of illegal Hispanic immigrants has decreased significantly from 2007. The number of unauthorized immigrants peaked in 2007 at 12 million and it has steadily declined since. This has been the first notable decrease, following two decades of steady growth. This falloff in the population of unauthorized immigrants has been mainly driven by a decrease in the number of new immigrants from Mexico, the largest source of U.S. migrants. The Pew Hispanic Center reports that the net immigration from Mexico to the U.S. has stopped and possibly reversed through 2010. The drop has been from 770,000 Mexican undocumented immigrants annually to an estimated 140,000, the majority who arrived as legal immigrants. This alone is an impressive shift.

The Latino Median Age

The Hispanic Institute and Americans for Secure Retirement collaborated to compose a study of who the Latinos are in America today. Their findings reported that the median age of

Hispanics is 27.3, compared to 39 years for non-Hispanic whites and 36.4 years for the U.S. as a whole. They also learned that more than twenty-five percent of Americans are in their preretirement years (ages forty-five to sixty-four), compared to just sixteen percent of the Hispanic population. Amazingly, more than twelve percent of the total U.S. population is aged sixty-five and older, while less than six percent of Hispanics fall into this range. As a whole, Latinos proved younger than the American population (The Hispanic Institute). Latino youthfulness makes them prime for the future.

Health and Longevity

Although Hispanics suffer from an array of diseases, they have proven to live longer than non-Hispanics. On average, Hispanics outlive whites by 2.5 years and blacks by 7.7 years, according to the report. Their life expectancy at birth in 2006 was 80.6 years, compared with 78.1 for whites, 72.9 for blacks and 77.7 years for the total population. There are two potential reasons for these outcomes 1) culture and lifestyle—support from extended family and weaker social ties (collectivist culture) and 2) migration—this is the "healthy migrate effect"—the belief is that when immigrants become ill, they return home to die in their homeland (Nasser). In this American culture where health is preached in every arena coupled with Latinos being younger, learning good health habits will marry longevity with good health making Latinos prime candidates for more years to stir the economy.

A Collective Society: All for One and One for All

Latino-Americans are from a culture whose values are strong regarding the concept of family—familismo—and the strong family ties and loyalty and the collective nature or collectivismo. While the U.S. cultivates independence, Latinos yearn to be with family and are interdependent. Respect, trust, and loyalty all stem from familismo (González & Benitez—Kindle Locations 331-332). Latinos have a difficult time conceptualizing independence from family and loved ones. These data reflect the first time that the National Center Health Services has released Hispanic life expectancy information. The data reports suggest that the codependence on family and friends may be what results in dependable and loyalty from the Hispanic population. I believe that their collectivism allows the Latino to be more connected to and understand the importance of agapáo love (doing the right thing because it *is* the right thing) and doing things for the good of others. Everything that Latinos do they do for the family and the community.

Education

The U.S. census reports that Hispanics tend to have lower educational levels than the U.S. population overall. Almost one-quarter of Hispanics over age 25, have less than a ninth grade education, compared to less than 7.41 percent of non-Hispanics in the U.S.. Latinos also lag behind the general population in post-high school education levels. Only nine percent of Hispanics have a bachelor's degree, compared to seventeen percent of the U.S. population (Llagos & Snyder). The rate of graduate or professional degrees earned decreased to 4.1 percent in this population (U.S. Census Bureau Briefing). This may be attributed to the language barrier, and the low socio-economic position of Latinos.

Although only nine percent of Hispanics have a bachelor's degree, eighty-nine percent of young adults believe a college education is important for success in life. Unfortunately, only about forty-eight percent plan to get a college degree (Pew Hispanic Center national survey). The results identify that the primary reason for this gap in higher education are their modest aspirations and financial pressures to support their families (Lopez). With the cost of higher education on a steady incline, most Hispanics are unable to reach their academic dreams. Understanding that Latinos are a collectivist culture, children feel the burden to financially contribute to the family rather than incur the expense of higher education.

The U.S. Census Bureau forecasts that by 2020, nearly one-in-four college-age adults will be Latino. However, because Latino students face unique obstacles (such as language barriers, low-socio economic positions, little encouragement from family and educators) in accessing and completing their education, they require specific, intentional support to reach their academic goals. Furthermore, their success is key for achieving the U.S. goal and ensuring the future of strong state economies (Camacho-Liu).

The Impact

More than 50.5 million strong and rapidly growing, Latinos are impacting every aspect of the national landscape, including popular culture, the food, the music, the workforce, consumerism, politics, and the American national identity. Latinos are emerging leaders because they possess the bilingual and bicultural skills needed for present state of globalization. The ability to speak Spanish has become a valuable commodity since Spanish is the second-most spoken language in the world at 325 million worldwide (www.about.com—Geography). Latinos, for the most part, have lived between two languages and two cultures and they have learned to synthesize both cultures and both languages effectively. This ability translates into the ability to assimilate to both worlds and move with ease from one to the other. A typical Hispanic family speaks English outside the home, Spanish in the home, and Spanglish (a merging of both languages) with friends and some family members. Latinos who are linguistically diverse, have a better chance of accessing higher education and creating businesses. Although most Latinos are not overtly aggressive they have recently created a silent surge that is empowering them as leaders. Latinos are now mainstreaming which has moved many to middle-class status.

Foresight: What is the Latino's Contribution to the U.S. Economy?

The Emergence of the Latino Middle-Class

For years, Latinos have been the invisible minority. Today these invisible Latinos have been absorbed into the mainstream. They have quietly gained force and have become an untold middle-class success that is hidden in plain sight and misunderstood (Chavez). Duncan, Hotz, and Trejo report that time and again researchers have found indicators that suggest labor market disadvantages for Hispanics, deficits such as employment gaps relative to Caucasian employees. This in part is explained by the low levels of human capital. What will transform the American job market are the essential skills that Hispanics possess in this globalized market. The one dimension that increases human capital is educational attainment.

The 2000 U.S. Census added a new and unexpected Latino geography—that of a Latino concentration in every state, reflecting a new dispersal trend outside the seven traditional states. This pattern has been coined *The Latino Diaspora*. There are two striking characteristics to this diaspora: a) Latino residential dispersal away from central city enclaves and into suburbia, small towns and nonmetropolitan areas and b) a more diverse population profile whereby Latinos are more likely to be migrants than immigrants. They also present a more complete spectrum of education, occupation, and income—a socioeconomic diversity that suggests the emergence of a new Latino middle class (Camayd-Freixas).

The median U.S. household income increased in the 2001 National Research Council survey from $31,470 (first-generation) to $40,505 (second-generation). When compared by ethnic group and second-generation, Puerto Ricans earned least with a household income of $36,989, Cubans the highest at $62,545, and South Americans immediately following at $52,085 (National Research Council). There has been huge improvement since this study; Latina women appear to spearhead this drastic change.

Rodriguez purports that this new group of Latino middle class members is comprised largely of a young, hard working, family-oriented Latino population who are accelerating their adaptation to changing economic conditions. This group has two sectors, the U.S.-born and foreign-born. These two groups are distinct, yet share primary values and behaviors. More than half the U.S.-born Latino households are rapidly achieving near-parity with the overall population. They are improving education levels and demonstrate increasingly successful integration into the burgeoning white-collar economy (Rodriguez, 1996).

It is clear that the growing trends in income have moved Latinos from low-socioeconomic stats to middle class, as Latinos have become educated and have upgraded their occupational status. Hispanic businesses are at the forefront of projecting the image of the middle-class Latino. For many years,

Latinos have been perceived as an economic burden; it's the view that constituted the rationale for challenging immigration and Latinos. But in 1994, (see reference) dedicated an issue to the coming out of the "silent minority," focusing on working-class recent immigrants, primarily Spanish language-speaking Hispanics, by highlighting the "silent minority" with enough power to exert influence in national and international politics (Dávila, 2008).

Emerging: Latino Professional

The number of Latinos with academic credentials has also been rising. Therefore, there is representation in an ever-widening variety of occupations. In 2009, the NCLR reported that there were 57,000 Hispanic physicians and surgeons, 202,000 middle-school teachers, 74,000 chief executives of businesses, 30,000 lawyers, and 284,000 firefighters. In 2010, nineteen percent of Hispanics worked in management and professional occupations (National Council of La Raza). Corporations are well aware of the rapidly growing Latino population. There are currently 44 million and growing projected to more than double to about 100 million by 2050. They are also aware of the estimates of the exodus from the workforce of retirees which will generate approximately 35 million job openings, with a growing crop of Hispanic candidates that will eventually fill many of those openings (Diversity MBA Magazine).

Emerging: Latino Business Ownership

There has been an unprecedented increase in Hispanic-owned Business; that continues to rise. The number of Hispanic-owned firms (defined as business where 51% or more of the equity stock is owned by Hispanics) has maintained a steady increase from 2002 (National Institute of La Raza). Business ownership has shifted the Latino population from what was for many years known as an indigenous population to into mainstream middle-class. The phenomenon is that Hispanics also lead in the increase of Business ownership.

Latino-owned business grew by forty-four percent, compared to eighteen percent for the rest of the nation (Minority Business Development Agency). In the west, Hispanic-owned business increased 47.1 percent (from 77,870 in 2002 to 114,592 in 2007). Nationally, the number of Hispanic business rose from 1.6 million in 2002 to 2.3 million in 2007, generating $345 billion in sales, a rise of 55.5 percent from 2002 (2010 U.S. Census Bureau). All other business increased from 23 million to 27.1 million, with only proportionate increases in business revenue.

The Latino-owned Business statistical increase is in non-farming Business. These businesses employ 1.9 million workers with a total payroll of $54.7 billion, an increase of twenty-six percent and forty-nine percent, respectively, since 2002. On average, however, Latino businesses made $153,000 a year, lower than the $179,000 average for minority-owned businesses, and slightly less than one third of the $490,000 average made by Caucasian-owned businesses.

Despite the impressive growth in sales in Latino-owned Business, they are predominately sole proprietorships with no employees. While Business ownership provides income and independence, it does not provide economic leadership in the community as well as better integration into the local, state and national economy. As a result, the overrepresentation of non-employer firms indicates barriers and challenges despite the recent growth patterns observed (The Julian Somora Research Institute).

Emerging: Buying Power

According to Glenn Llopis, contributor to Forbes Magazine, Latinos in the U.S. are not valued enough by America's corporations, government, or mainstream media. He points out that brand marketers do not take Latino customers' buying power or trend-setting influence seriously enough. Advertisers underestimate the importance of the Hispanics as an economic and Business development engine (Forbes.com). According to the Neilson report the Hispanic buying power is an annual $1.0 trillion and expected to grow to $1.5 trillion over the next five years (Neilson, 2012; Nahn, 2012).

The Problem: Where Do We Go From Here. . .

Despite the continuous growth of Latinos in areas such as education, professions, and Business, Latinos continue to have extraordinary obstacles in each of these defining areas. The underline complication is finances. Since most Latinos are now just beginning to transition from low socioeconomic status to middle-class the pursuit of education is not always at the top of the list.

A significant obstacle to Latino Business growth, according to the Texas study, is lack of management and leadership skills and the need for improved Business relations and more effective communication. Bruce Kellison of the Bureau of Business Research (BBR), an associate director and coauthor of the study, reports that "the key training needs issues were surprising because they were about running the company and motivating employees, not the nuts and bolts issues of accounting or lack of capital found in most minority Business literature." (Bureau of Business Research).

The Solution: Making the Logical Choice

The one thing that distinguishes Latinos is their innate ability to work hard, be dependable, show loyalty, and have integrity. These alone are marketable attributes, but if we add to this the idea that a bicultural, bilingual, and collective society that is wired to survive in difficult, fast-changing times, they are ripe for the shift in leadership. According to Llopis, Hispanic leaders operate from these characteristics:

➢ An understanding of uncertainty and change from reform and revolution

➢ An understanding of reinvention from being misrepresented

➢ An understanding of personal branding as they begin to live passionately for those things they stand for

➢ A perspective that makes them uniquely capable of surviving and thriving in the new workplace

➢ They represent one of the fastest growing groups of entrepreneurs in the U.S.

The solution relies on offering Latino leaders in the workforce and Business what they KNOW they need and not what others THINK they need. Latinos are ripe for this shift in leadership; they have been an invisible people who have been silently preparing for this shift. The *one essential* thing for elevating a population is education. And Latinos are becoming more proactive in pursuing higher education. Diverse Education stated that the Pew Research Center's Hispanic Trends Project, reported that for the first time in history there were higher education enrollment rates in Latino high school graduates than that of White high school graduates (Roach, 2013). The shift in economic status, allowing Latinos to achieve the American dream and that is higher education. This change is repositioning

Latino socio economic status. Latinos need to understand their history and foresee their potential.

With adequate training, guidance, nurture, and refinement, Latinos are changing the landscape of corporate America. Some may even say that Latinos are single handedly saving American corporations (Llopis, 2013). The current whirlwind in 21st century globalization makes the Latino the most logical choice for leadership. This book covers the fundamental areas where Latinos not only have the potential for becoming the next group of global and business leaders, but they actually have the innate skill set for leadership. We will cover each area where Latinos already possess the basic competencies that will stimulate them to be catalytic in business leadership. This book is designed to assist in the professional development of Latino entrepreneurs and established companies that wish to take advantage of "The Leadership Shift" and *Strategically Positioning themselves as Business Leaders.*"

"A great leader's courage to fulfill his vision comes from passion, not position."
John Maxwell

Chapter 2

Emotional Intelligence in Latino Leadership

Today there is a lot of talk about Emotional Intelligence and the importance of EI to business. There is training, and companies are expressing an interest in evaluating employee EI scores. For many years, intelligence was evaluated through Intelligence Quotient (IQ) testing. It was never considered that an individual's level of IQ was a conglomeration of environment, upbringing, culture, and personal experiences. As a result, IQ scores varied significantly by ethnic group, socioeconomic levels, and physical environment.

The IQ evaluation tool was being questioned by theorist who believed that it may be flawed and that possibly other things must be considered when calculating intelligence. IQ testing and the varying scores began brewing debate for many sociologists and psychother-apists, igniting theories that ques-tioned the intelligence measuring tool—which resulted in the gen-esis of what we now call EI/EQ. Although it would seem that

"It is very important to understand that emotional intelligence is not the opposite of intelligence, it is not the triumph of heart over head,—it is the unique intersection of both."

David Caruso

currently, Emotional Quotient (EQ) is all the rage, this idea has

"Social intelligence involves one's ability to understand and interpret social situations as well as interact appropriately."

Edward Thorndike

been a topic of interest for many years. Let's dissect EI/EQ and explore what it is, how it was developed, the impact it has on leadership style, and where Latino leaders place as a group in EQ scores.

The Evolution of Emotional Intelligence

Although the term "EI" may be new, the idea of Emotional Intelligence can be traced to the 1920s when Edward Thorndike, a sociologist, identified the art of interpersonal relationships. The study and measurement of EI has its roots in the work of such psychometric pioneers as Binet, Thorndike, and Wechsler (Fancher, 1985). Thorndike developed an interest in researching the interaction of levels-of-emotion with levels-of-intelligence. He proposed three distinct types of intelligence: 1) abstract, 2) mechanical, and 3) social. Over many years, social intelligence has remained a topic of interest but it was not until 1990 that it was revisited with renewed interest.

In the 1960s, Van Ghent and Leuner (1966) coined the term *"Emotional Intelligence"* as an aside in literary criticism. Two decades later, Payne (1986) employed EI more extensively in his dissertation. In the 1990s, Mayer, Salovey, and Caruso wrote articles that developed and defined the theory and demonstrated a measurement of EI. They editorialized it for further study (Mayer, Salovey, Caruso, 2004). But Goleman ignited the momentum of the *"emotional intelligence"* philosophy to a wide audience with his book *Emotional Intelligence.* Goleman merged the concept with business in his 1998 Harvard Business Review article Goleman researched nearly two hundred companies globally and learned that the qualities traditionally associated with leadership, such as intelligence, toughness, determination, and vision required for success are insufficient (Goleman, HBR 1998).

Emotional Intelligence Defined

EI is regarded a member of a class of intelligences including social, practical, and personal intelligences, now called the "hot intelligence." This label indicates that these intelligences operate on hot cognitions—cognitions dealing with matters of personal, emotional importance to the individual (Mayer, Salovey and Caruso, 2004).

EI is the measure of how one develops the capacity to reason about emotions and of the emotions that enhance mindset. Emotional intelligence (EI) represents the ability to validly reason with emotions and use emotions to enhance thought. According to Mayer, Salovey, and Caruso, EI is the ability to recognize the meanings of emotion and their relationships, and to reason and problem-solve using emotions. It involves the capacity to perceive emotions, assimilate emotion-related feelings, understand the information of those emotions, and manage them.

To understand the core of the meaning of Emotional Intelligence, let's take it apart and examine the pieces. Emotion refers to a feeling state (including physiological responses and cognitions) that conveys information about relationships. Intelligence refers to the capacity to reason validly about information. When these two words are combined, the term *emotional intelligence* is consistent with scientific literature in the fields of intelligence, personality psychology, and emotions (Mayer, Salovey, and Caruso).

The Philosophies

The Mayer and Salovey EI Philosophy:

In 1990, Mayer and Salovey created the EI philosophy as a four-branch model of emotional intelligence: Perception, Reasoning, Understanding, and Managing. **Perception** of the emotion is the first branch of the knowledge received by observing the mannerisms and expressions of the body. In this branch, the perception of emotions gives one the capacity to recognize emotions through facial and body expressions. It expresses the ability to decipher nonverbal communication in the face, voice, and other, related channels. Body language is a form of perceiving emotion and it accounts for fifty-five percent of all communication.

Reasoning, the second branch, helps us deal more effectively with anger, by making the individual responsible for the appropriateness and expression of one's emotions. *Reasoning* is a way to bridge the thought process and the way the brain processes emotions or cognitive actions. Human beings are ruled by emotions; emotions dictate how we respond and react to the world around us. With appropriate reasoning of emotions, you will learn to apply positive action and curtail negative emotions.

Branch 3 is *Understanding* the emotions. You will find that these four branches build on each other; perception and reasoning are but a small part of the self-awareness process. EI helps build on interpreting emotions through perception, which builds on reasoning and again on understanding. The only way for people to deal properly with their emotions is to **understand** them. Even when an individual expresses emotions inappropriately, such as in anger, you don't want to perceive what they are experiencing. You want to take the time to understand the reason behind the eruption so you can assist in teaching a different way to handle that emotion. It is important to understand that emotions can come from stress or frustration and not necessarily because they are angry with you.

The last is to *Manage* emotions. This final branch to EI focuses on the managing of emotions or to present an appropriate response to one's and others' emotions. There are emotions everywhere around us, what we now call "drama."

Although not all emotion is dramatic or negative, everyone has emotions even if they are internalized. Emotions, we now understand, can be learned—acquired through observation—while others can be innate or cultural.

These four branches of emotional intelligence are critical to comprehending the depth of emotional competence in you and in your staff. EQ is having self-awareness connected with the emotions connected with self-awareness, self-assessment accuracy, and self-confidence (Allen, 2013).

> *"If your emotional abilities aren't in hand, if you don't have self-awareness, if you are not able to manage your distressing emotions, if you can't have empathy and have effective relationships, then no matter how smart you are, you are not going to get very far."*
>
> *Daniel Goleman*

The Goleman EI Philosophy:

In 1995, Daniel Goleman introduced another level to EI by proposing that transformational leaders exhibit five essential competencies: self-awareness, self-regulation, social skill, empathy, and motivation. These skills are not necessarily innate competencies, but are learned capabilities that must be developed to achieve ultimate performance.

Emotions can grow only if given attention and allowed to play out freely. Without attention, emotions such as anger will die. Given attention, they can make us do things that may even be out of character. Although all emotions need an outlet, how, when, and where we allow the emotion loose will make a difference (Goleman, 1995). He further notes that the concept of IQ over EQ, or conventional intelligence, is far too narrow and wider areas of EI dictate and enable one's level of success.

In today's world, success requires much more than IQ, the measure by which levels of success have been measured. Ignoring essential behavioral and character elements is now the greater measure. An individual can be academically brilliant yet suffer social and interpersonal ineptness. While it has been proven that high IQ does not ensure great success, nevertheless, high EQ has been proven to ensure great success. The premise is that EQ ensures success, and requires the effective awareness, control, and management of one's own emotions, and those of others.

EQ embraces two aspects of intelligence: first, understanding yourself, your goals, intentions, responses, and behavior; and second, understanding others and their feelings (Goleman; BusinessBall.com).

Bar-On Creates the Measurement Tool:

In 2006, a tool was created to measure Emotional Intelligence levels—created by Reuven Bar-On and named *"The Emotional Quotient Inventory (EQ-i), EQ-360 and EQ-i: YV."* These measurement tools were developed to assess the Bar-On model of emotional-social intelligence. It is a self-report measurement, designed to measure several constructs related to EI; it consists of 133 items, and takes approximately thirty minutes to complete. The scores give an overall EQ score as well as scores for each of the following five composite scales and fifteen subscales (Bar-On, 2006).

The EQ-i Composite Scales and Subscales

INTRAPERSONAL (self-awareness and self-expression)

> ➢Self-Regard: To accurately perceive, understand, and accept oneself.

> ➢Emotional Self-Awareness: To be aware of and understand one's emotions.

> ➢Assertiveness: To effectively and constructively express one's emotions and oneself.

> ➢Independence: To be self-reliant and free of emotional dependency on others.

> ➢Self-Actualization: To strive to achieve personal goals and actualize one's potential.

INTERPERSONAL (social awareness and interpersonal relationships)

> ➢Empathy: To be aware of and understand how others feel.

> ➢Social Responsibility: To identify with one's social group and cooperate with others.

➢Interpersonal Relationship: To establish mutually satis-fying relationships and relate well with others.

STRESS MANAGEMENT (emotional management and regulation)

➢Stress Tolerance: To effectively and constructively manage emotions.

➢Impulse Control: To effectively and constructively control emotions.

ADAPTABILITY (change management)

➢Reality-Testing: To objectively validate one's feelings and thinking with external reality.

➢Flexibility: To adapt and adjust one's feelings and thinking to new situations.

➢Problem-Solving: To solve effectively problems of a personal and interpersonal nature.

GENERAL MOOD (self-motivation)

➢Optimism: To be positive and look at the brighter side of life.

➢Happiness: To feel content with oneself, others and life in general (Bar-On, 2006).

Correlation between EI Competency and Brain Function

Goleman identified EI competency as the fundamental for outstanding leadership. *Primal Leadership* explains that breakthroughs in brain research explain why leaders' moods and actions have enormous impact on those they lead. The research identifies the power of emotionally intelligent leadership that inspires, arouses passion and enthusiasm, and keeps people motivated and committed. Conversely, toxic leadership has the polar opposite effect in that it poisons the emotional climate of a workplace. Each has the power to affect the environment through different perspectives of the task (Goleman, Boyatzis, and McKee, 2002). Dr. Caroline Leaf reports that every thought has a corresponding electrochemical reaction in the brain. At any given moment, the brain is creatively performing about a billion actions, of which of which you are conscious only of about 2,000. Brain detoxification determines one's attitude toward life, which directly reflects your state of mind. She reports that the brain releases chemical secretions causing either positive or negative thoughts. There is a direct connection between one's thought life and one's body. She proposes a brain detoxification as necessary to discard toxic thoughts and emotions (Leaf, 2007). Brain researchers have identified distinct circuitry for emotional intelligence

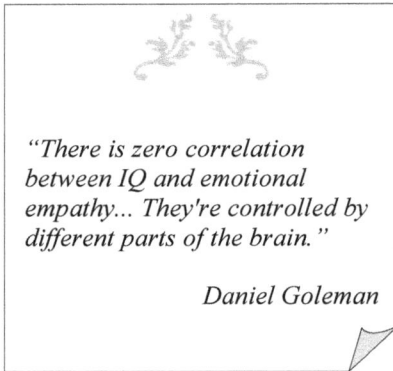

> *"There is zero correlation between IQ and emotional empathy... They're controlled by different parts of the brain."*
>
> *Daniel Goleman*

milestones. The Bar-On EQ-i:S instrument studies EI competencies and has one of the more convincing proofs that emotional intelligence resides in brain areas distinct from those for IQ. The data supports the premise that there are unique brain centers that govern emotional intelligence, which distinguishes this set of human skills from academic (that is, verbal, math, and spatial) intelligence—or IQ, as these purely cognitive skills are known—as well as from personality traits (Goleman, 2011).

This theory endorses the premise that leaders with high EQ scores are emotionally self-aware, attuned to their inner signals. (Goleman, Boyatzis, and McKee, 2002):

➢ They maintain self-control and manage their disturbing emotions and impulses.

➢ They are transparent and live their values.

➢ They have empathy and are aware of a wide range of emotional signals.

➢ They have organizational awareness, social awareness, are politically astute, read key power relationships, and are inspirational.

➢ They create resonance and motivate with a compelling vision, they influence, develop others by cultivating people abilities.

➢They are change catalysts, great at conflict resolution, generating teamwork and collaboration.

Emotional constructs in leadership has been a much-researched topic for decades. That explains the relationship between positive moods and charismatic leadership, emotional management and transformational leadership, emotional expression and leader member exchange. It also explains a leader's emotional displays and followership behavior, (Jordan & Troth, 2010) and high organization performance and servant leadership (Melchar & Bosco, 2010). Then there is the head and heart leadership style coined Servant Leadership. Servant leadership models high emotional competence and may predispose leaders to adopt a relationship-oriented leadership style, as illustrated in the servant leadership theory (Hannay & Fretwell). This model shows the balance necessary to obtain SL status, such as Education, Social, Physical, Family, and Spiritual health = a servant leader.

The Influence EI has on Leadership

Taking into account the philosophies of Mayer, Salovey, Caruso, and Goleman, let's review two leadership styles that have been correlated with high EQ scores. In a study done by Mills, she reports that the concept of transformational leadership may provide a model for the relevance of emotions to leadership. She cites Bass and Avolio's four dimensions of transformational leadership: idealized influence, inspirational motivation, intellectual stimulation, and individualized consideration. These leadership skills, Mills proposes, may be considered intertwined with the concepts of emotional intelligence. The results of the study, Mill's reports, suggest that EI may now be considered a component of leadership effectiveness. This is no longer a soft skill; therefore, implementing a leadership style in practice that is reflective of EI may support greater levels of leadership effectiveness (Mills, 2009).

Another leadership style that proves to have high EI is Servant Leadership. Many theorists propose that the quintessential leader is the servant leader. For instance, Hannay and Fretwell report that the servant leadership theory goes beyond traditional trait, behavioral, and situational theories and completely changes the focus of the leader. A servant leader does not view the position as a way to fulfill his/her own needs; rather uses the position to focus on meeting the needs of their followers (employees). This kind of leadership style is unique and selfless and requires an individual who is willing to place the focus on promoting others. The authors propose that employees with high EI are more likely to adapt to the servant leadership style and are more effective at managing their own emotions and their relationships with others (Hannay & Fretwell). EI has been found to influence transformational leadership traits (Gardner & Stough, 2002).

The pioneer of the servant leadership model was Robert Greenleaf in the 1970s. Today, Bruce Winston and Kathleen Patterson have also done extensive research on SL and allude to the correlation between EI and Servant Leadership qualities. EI was found to have a positive impact on leader self-esteem and emotional well-being (Parolini, 2005). Winston proposes that there appears to be a relative application of EI to servant leadership concept. The relationship of EI constructs and servant leadership model bear very impressive similarities. To name a few:

> In the EI model, it appraises and expresses emotion to enhance cognitive processes;

> Page & Wong's SL Model: caring for others, integrity, authentic, visioning, goal;

> Patterson SL Model: Trust, Altruism, service to follower, agapáo love, humility and vision;

> Russell & Stone SL Model: trust, appreciation, integrity, credibility, persuasion and, influence;

> Sendjaya & Sarros SL Model: authentic self, equality, trust, self-awareness, self-perception and vision;

> Winston's SL Model: commitment to the leader, trust, altruism, service to the leader, agapáo love and service (Winston & Hartsfield, 2004).

"Agapáo" is the Greek word that defines a leader who does the right thing for the right reason; to love in a social moral sense; and having moral values that can only be obtained through agapáo leadership. In a rapidly changing world, servant leadership will be the only pragmatic way to lead companies. Followers of all walks will follow only those who care about their best interests. To the extent that this servant leadership principle prevails in the future, the only truly viable institutions will be those that are predominantly servant-led (Greenleaf).

Emotional Intelligence and Cross-Cultural Leadership Effectiveness

We've discussed the intelligence quotient, emotional quotient and now we will explore the cultural quotient. Cultural intelligence or Cultural Quotient (CQ) is yet another intelligence capacity that is consistent with modern conceptualizations of intelligence—it recognizes that intelligence is far more than general mental capacity. By understanding different types of intelligences, we can differentiate specific proficiencies that have relevance in varying situations (Livermore, 2010).

Defining CQ

The global international economic borders continue to be pushed back, resulting in not only the global exchange of goods and services, but just as important, the exchange of human resources (Vij, 2011). The globalized world requires that businesses operate increasingly in interconnectedness. The competition is just as close. The 21st century will continue to increase important business opportunities that will exist outside the headquarters country. As the business world becomes increasingly globalized, this does not mean that cultural differences will diminish. The success of the business and profitability overseas will rely greatly on the quality of effective global leaders and based on those results, 85 percent of U.S. Fortune 500 firms believe they currently do not have an adequate number of global leaders to sustain global operations (Reilly & Karounos). You will find that the most efficient global leaders will be those who score high in CQ (cognitive intelligence) and focus on specific proficiencies that are important for high quality personal relationships and effectiveness in culturally diverse settings (Livermore).

We are now living in the information age, where advancements in the field of information and communications technology have contributed substantially to this rising trend of interconnected businesses and the remarkable growth of the multinational and transformational corporations (Vij, 2011). Therefore, it is imperative that we understand the need to merge emotional intelligence (EI) with cultural intelligence (CQ).

Emphasizing the Importance for EI and CQ Awareness

Understanding the relevance of IQ vs. EQ was a great triumph in understanding human and social behavior. Nevertheless, there was still a missing component—understanding how to merge EQ with CQ. Cultural intelligence (CQ) is defined as a person's ability to function effectively in situations characterized by cultural diversity (Lugo). By measuring and examining the degree to which emotional intelligence (EQ) and cultural intelligence (CQ), self- and social dimension skills are related to transformational leadership self- and social dimension skills. This study examined the existence, or lack thereof, of a positive relationship between emotional and cultural intelligence and the self- and social dimensions of transformational leadership.

The premise of self-dimension skills is to examine the individual skills and behaviors that affect an individual's relationship with self; whereas social dimension skills identified the individual skills and behaviors that affect a person's relationship with others (Goleman, 1995). Despite the extensive research done on EI, researchers have noted that there is still a deficit in addressing a person's multicultural understanding and their ability to succeed in different cultural environments. Some theorists assert that EI can predict success if an individual understands how to function within specific cultural environment theories. Such dynamics, according to Early and Ang, lead to the development of a theory of cultural intelligence. What constitutes culture or cultural "syndromes" are the specific characteristics shared by a group of people and they result from the common denominators of society, such as regional location, language, generation, religion, or political experience. CQ provides insights about an individual's ability to cope in multicultural situations, engage in cross-cultural interactions, and perform in culturally diverse work groups (Lugo).

Melding EQ and CQ in Global Leadership

Two things are inevitable: first, that globalization is on the rise, global interaction will become the norm, and second, that leadership people must prepare for global leadership tasks. Behavior is largely influenced by cultural background. At one time, becoming a global leader specifically meant that one was relocating as a business leader or missionary. Today global leadership may be domestic. Since Columbus, the US has been a 'melting pot' of cultures, but today the there is a shift in cultures that often makes those of second and third generations uncomfortable, not to mention the international interaction. But it seems that for the most part, interactions between cultures are at best off to a hot rough start (PearsonHigherEd.com).

> *"Cultural intelligence offers leaders an overall repertoire and perspectives that can be applied to a myriad of cultural situations."*
>
> David Livermore

A person's behavior is greatly influenced by a cultural background. As a result, leadership must use the EQ to run its organizations successfully, both domestic and global, as a unified entity. Emotional competence is essential to global business leaders. There are organizations that customize their business approach and business policies according to the cultural needs of that particular market. Companies with high CQ computations shape the preparation of global teams to match the needs of that culture. Rewards, incentives, and any motivational tools must be designed in view of the cultural ethos of the particular geographical territory. Today there is an increase in the number of multinational corporations that account for a significant share of the world's industrial investment, production, and employment trade. There are thousands of patent firms, with hundreds of thousands of foreign affiliates, that employee people globally (TrainingZone.co/uk). There is no question but that the future will increasingly demand for global leaders who are proficient in both EQ and CQ.

Cultural intelligence is imperative in this global market. Fortune 500 companies have become aware that they have a shortfall of global leaders, yet they are still uncertain about exactly how to develop such leadership. The diversity training activities currently implemented are at best deficient. The obstacle for organizations is the lack of authenticity in how they integrate cultural intelligence into their business model, because it makes leaders uncomfortable. What is now happening is that business leaders are recognize a shift: organizations are losing business to small businesses that are Latino-owned. They are also losing diverse members of their workforce to the same competitors because they severely lack the cultural intelligence to keep them (Llopis, 2011).

How EQ and CQ Translates into Latino Leadership

According to the research, business success leaders must exhibit high EQ scores. Simultaneously, with rapid change and global interaction, high CQ scores are equally as important. EQ and CQ are similar because both have capabilities thought to be important to both personal and professional success. Success in the 21st century globalized economy will appeal for EQ and CQ awareness and the ability to acclimate to various cultures (Livermore). Diversity, complexities, and international com-petition and having leaders who are capable of understanding, functioning, and managing in the global environment will be an in inimitable commodity that offers companies an outstanding competitive advantage (Ang & Inkpen, 2008; Barney, 1992).

In a study done of a group of Latin Americans, African American, Whites, and Mexicans, EI was measured through the Trait Meta-Mode Scale. The key facets of emotional intelligence that were explored were Attention, Clarity, and Repair:

> ➤*Attention* conveys the degree to which individuals tend to observe and think about their feelings and moods.

> ➤*Clarity* evaluates the propensity to discriminate between emotions and moods.

> ➤*Repair* is the tendency to regulate one's feelings.

The findings were:

➢*Attention*—Mexicans reported lower scores. African Americans, Latinos, and Whites were notably higher. Whites were higher than African Americans and Latinos.

➢*Clarity*—the scores reported significant differences among ethnic groups. Mexicans revealed lower scores than African Americans, Latinos, and Whites. Latinos had the overall highest scores.

➢The *Repair* subscale reported no significant differences among ethnic groups.

There can be an array of hypotheses for the outcomes, but a conceivable explanation for this discrepancy may be cultural differences in value systems. According to theorists, when contrasting the cultural dimension of individualism versus collectivism, individualism is defined as a person's emotional and autonomous independence towards groups or organizations. Collectivism describes dependence on groups of which the individual becomes a part. Societal groups such as Latinos who espouse collectivism are found to focus less attention on individual emotions and more on the needs of the group, as a result their EQ scores tend to be higher.

EQ + CQ = Latino Business Leader

Goleman was responsible for the merging of EI and business. He understood that to be "the leader of the pack," a leader must exhibit high EQ levels. The management of emotions is the core essence of leadership. If one can manage and control personal emotions, one learns to manage the emotions of others. Organizations are recognizing that EI is essential part of a company's management process. Currently the emphasis is on team building and adapting to change, therefore EI becomes even more critical to the process (Cook, 1998). As the future unfolds, it will become more evident to organizational leaders that they will be effective only if they learn to deal effectively with emotions, their own, and the emotions of others (Goleman, Boyatzis, & McKee, 2002). The 21st century business has changed and it now requires an elevated state of intelligence that encompasses work perform-ance and EQ scores in leadership in the business world. This was the essence of Goleman's studies in 1995 and 1998.

Leaders with high EI scores have the characteristics that determine the ability to inspire followers to commit to a shared vision and goals. This is done by challenging them to be innovative problem solvers and develop followers' leadership capacity through mentoring and providing challenge and support. Cross-cultural research has demonstrated that cultural values among Hispanics are significantly different from non-Hispanic Whites.

Still, other research has demonstrated that these bi-cultural experiences assist Hispanic Americans to function effectively in two cultures. Corona cites Torres as asserting that Latino

Americans have the ability to employ a different set of skills necessary to be effective in both US mainstream and Hispanic cultures. Latino Americans form their identities in terms of behaviors, values, and norms associated with bicultural experiences (Corona, 2009). Latino leaders must not only be empathetic but must also comprehend and appreciate cultural pluralism. This new generation of Latino leaders require new knowledge, skills, and abilities, as they face a constantly changing and borderless global marketplace. Therefore, emotional intelligence (EI), cross-cultural adjustment, cross-cultural awareness (CQ), and managing cross-cultural conflict is identified as some of the global competencies needed by global leaders. This will be the only way to compete effectively in this global marketplace (Lugo). Latinos are ready to bridge this gap since they are proficient in multicultural interactions.

The Business Journal of Hispanic Research presented a study executed by Miguel A. Corona. The study samples were Hispanic Americans, and tests were Bar-On's EQ-i:S and Bass & Riggio's MLQ-5X (which examines transformational leadership skills). The findings were that Hispanics are significantly more attuned to managing their own emotions and those of others. These results are supported by previous research indicating Hispanics demonstrate high levels of communication and social skills. This, Corona indicates, is due to being from a collectivist culture that values relationships over personal needs. Research has supportive evidence that Hispanics emphasize the building of emotional bonds (*confianza*) that increase camaraderie and cooperation (Bordas, 1999). The overall study strongly suggests that Latinos possess the EI characteristics necessary to establish strong workplace relationships (Corona, 2010).

The Time is Ripe for Latino Leadership

Latinos are ripe for the shift in leadership, and the shift is due to the growing numbers of Latino population. It is also because Latinos possess the capacity for global interaction, making them the logical choice for global leadership. As we examined in Chapter 1, the Latino history, the forming trends and the future increase in the Latino population and its multicultural nature is setting the stage for future Latino leadership. In this segment we uncovered EI and how much more important EQ is over IQ (Mayer, Salovey, Caruso, Goleman). We learned that IQ levels are based on academic levels, socioeconomic standards, and personal experiences, environmental and social exposure. Most Latinos fall miles behind because they struggle with language barriers and socioeconomic poverty. They live in barrios, and therefore their education is substandard.

According to the EQi Meta Scales, Latinos score higher than White Americans. My hypothesis: it is due to differences in individualism and collectivism, which play a significant role in EQi scores. Americans are an individualist society, and as a result, are inclined to be more selfish, blame others, lay guilt, exaggerate or minimize feelings, lack integrity and sense of conscience, carry grudges, act out feelings, play games, are indirect and evasive, lack empathy, are rigid and inflexible, not emotionally available, poor listeners, defensive and believe in self rather than God.

They may also experience low self-esteem, poor self-confidence, may be apathetic, and have difficulty expressing love for others. American's EQi scores are usually low. Latinos who are from a collective society have the inclination to have high EQi scores. They are maintain self-control and manage their disturbing emotions and impulses. The Latino's regard for respect of others is catalyst in their aggregate EQ. They are transparent and live their values. They are empathetic and are aware of a wide range of emotional signals. They have social awareness, and are not motivated by wealth, status, fame, or approval. They are emotionally resilient, optimistic yet realistic, do not internalize failure, care about others' feelings and read key power relationships, and are spiritual with strong beliefs in God. It would seem that collectivism is synonymous with high EQi scores.

There was also discussion on CQ scores and the need for cultural intelligence competencies in this globalized marketplace (Livermore). Most Latinos have lived in a multicultural world with very close connections to their native land, language, and culture. Latinos are prepared for global interaction, since it is innate. Despite generational distance, Latinos are connected to their roots and have loyalties to both their native Latin American country as well as America. They sympathize as 100 percent

Latino-Americano and 100 percent American. They live between two bridges (this will be discussed in depth in upcoming chapters). Latinos cultural competence is leap years ahead of Americans due to their multicultural identification.

In this rapidly increasing globalization, the requirement calls for a new generation of leaders who have a high degree of emotional and cultural competency. Latinos are the consummate contenders. It is imperative that Latino leaders not only be empathetic but also comprehend and appreciate cultural pluralism so they and their firms can adapt to new cultures. In order to succeed, this new generation of leaders should acquire new knowledge, skills, and abilities, as they face a constantly changing and borderless global marketplace. Emotional intelligence, cross-cultural adjustment, cross-cultural awareness, and managing cross-cultural conflict has been identified as some of the global competencies needed by leaders, in order to compete effectively in a global marketplace (Vance & Paik, 2006).

At a distance, we can hear the thunder of an economic globalized marketplace that exhibits the capacity to identify and cultivate effective leaders from among a culturally diverse labor pool that is becoming a competitive demand (Corona). There are Latinos entering leadership positions at an unprecedented rate. Organizations must ensure that they value the knowledge, skills, and abilities that Latinos provide. Those companies that provide opportunities for advancement, leadership development, and training that offers material of cultural relevance to the Hispanic experience are positioning themselves for future success (Johnson & Negron, 2009). The Hispanic population in the US is uniquely positioned to play a more defined leadership role both domestically and internationally. Some believe that Latino leadership will actually save corporate America (Llopis, 2013). There is a notable increase in Hispanics who are accessing, reconstructing, and leading existing and newly created socioeconomic systems, structures, and institutions. Therefore, it is imperative that Latinos build upon their distinctive leadership abilities and methods to be effective when it is their turn to lead (Ramirez, 2006). It is time that Latinos stand up and acknowledge their positions and their preparation as leaders. It is essential that Latinos become trained and educated so they are prepared for the passing of the leadership torch. Latino, you are much more prepared for this trans-formation than they are aware.

There is very limited research done on the emotional intelligence, cultural intelligence, and global leadership in the Hispanic population. It behooves researchers to explore the EQ and CQ of Latino population. This population that is growing so rapidly and forecasted to increase to one-third of the U.S. population by 2050, and the fact that Latinos have bi-cultural and bi-lingual proficiency and the potential for global leadership roles merits the research in the EQ and CQ of Latinos.

Chapter 3
Core Beliefs, Ethics, and Values That Shape Latino Businesses

So what is the genesis of values? Prior to the nineteenth century, the word "values" was never used outside the economics context. Since then, values and morals have become the philosophical measure by which individuals and groups are evaluated (Joas, 2000), and have been coined in the single term: "cultural values." Cultural values are the official and external imposition of shared values that determine patriotism, national identity, national threat, citizenship, legality or non-legality, what is crime, and what is encouraged or discouraged on a constitutional national level in national government and all its institutions (Young, 2009).

> *"The quality of a person's life is in direct proportion to their commitment to excellence, regardless of their chosen field of endeavor."*
>
> *Vince Lombardi*

When defining Latino cultural values, we include individuals who are from Spanish-speaking countries. These include Cuban, Mexico, Puerto Rico, South and Central America. While there are notable differences in dialect, geopolitical, generations and acculturation/assimilation experiences, customs, traditions, economic resources, and educational systems, all Latinos share similar family values (Leon, 2010). To gain an appreciation for any culture, it is essential to understand its values. This exploration will yield astounding insight into who Latinos are. In this segment, we will explain the richness of the Latino heritage that will uncover an understanding of the Latino cultural design. Its review will bridge Chapter 2 with this segment of the series.

Chapter 2 clearly indicated that Latinos exhibit high levels of emotional intelligence. It also disclosed the findings from the Bar-On's EQ-i:S and Bass & Riggio's MLQ-5X (which examines transformational leadership skills). The research revealed that Hispanics are significantly more attuned to managing their own and others' emotions. Other research findings propose that Hispanics demonstrate high levels of communication and social skill. We will now explore how the Hispanic personal and collective values, morals, and ethics are instrumental in shaping Latino business leaders.

Values, Ethics, Morals Defined

Values are the rules by which we make decisions about right and wrong, the "should and should not," and the "good and the bad." Values measure the relative importance of one fact over another. Values are founded on the beliefs of the person or social group in which the individual has made an emotional investment. Values can be very conservative or loose and opposing (Dictionary.com).

Morals, in most cultures, have a greater social basis than values and tend to have a broader acceptance. Morals are more about right and wrong, good or bad, than values. We judge others more harshly on morals than on values, to the degree that we describe a person as immoral. There is no word for the absence of values. Motivation is founded on ideas of right and wrong (Dictionary.com).

Ethics is defined in business terms. There are professional ethics but rarely professional morals. Ethics is codified into a formal system or set of rules that are adopted by a group of people. In professions such as medical, psychological, finance, etc., there are codes of ethics. Ethnics are internally defined and adopted, whereas, morals are externally imposed. Calling an individual unethical is equal to calling them unprofessional, often an offensive insult. Ethics is a theory of moral values governing the conduct of a profession (Dictionary.com).

In defining values and ethics, realize how they are the framework on which good character is built. Without values, it is virtually impossible to have morals; great morals formulate good character, which predicates ethical principles that governs the individual. Having high ethical standards is solely for the professional, any person whether employee or leader wants to model excellent ethical integrity.

Exploring Latino Core Cultural Values

Stereotypes are formed from a person's or group's uninformed judgment of about another cultural group. The stereotype of Latinos is that they are too passive and lack the conviction to be good managers; or that Latinos are too emotional to fulfill leadership roles (Rodriguez, 2008). Remember, the EQ-i:S and the MLQ-5X, scored effectively negate those stereotypes. These unfounded stereotypes are the lack of comprehension of how cultural principles and traditions affect actions and behaviors.

Although it is often dangerous to generalize about cultural groups, it is also important to make well-informed observations about a culture to understand it. Observations such as the group's values, morals, and ethics are essential in understanding the group or individual. There are, for instance, certain characteristic values in the Hispanic culture that can be contrasted with equivalent elements of the Anglo culture. By comprehending these core values, one can avoid making erroneous judgments of Hispanics and will increase effect-tiveness when building the bridge of communication (Erickson, 2009). If you attempt to separate values and morals from the Latino culture, you will discover no culture at all. The Latino culture is regulated by its values, morals, and ethical standards, without which there *is* no Latino culture. The core values, morals, and standards of the Hispanic culture are best defined by interpreting how they have been shaped.

Values and Morals Begin in la Iglesia:

For more than five centuries, the Latino culture has been shaped by a unique set of historical circumstances. The formation of Latino values begins with religion. When the Spanish colonized Latin America they brought with them clergymen whose mission was to spread Catholicism. History and tradition has created a strong disposition toward religion and spirituality (Rodriguez).

Core values in the Latino culture stem from '*la iglesia*' (the church). The values are built around the fear of, respect for, and wrath of God. Doing right means gaining a blessing; doing wrong is a certain curse. Although most Latinos are Catholic Christians, most of those with different faiths also believe in God. The direction, guidance, education, and raising of children comes from the church.

Depending on the region, Latinos may look to alternative healthcare providers such as curaderos (healers), sobadores (chiropractors), espiritistas (spiritual healer) or santaria (the occult) (Pajewski & Enriquez, 1996).

Another essential value for Latinos is the gender-specific *Marianismo,* which also stems from Catholicism. This value strongly encourages young Latinas to look to the Virgin Mary as a role model for the ideal woman. Latinas are encouraged to maintain celibacy be spiritually strong, nurturing and self-sacrificing (Lopez-Baez,1999).

The Values and Morals in el Familismo

Familismo is highly regarded and valued in the Latino culture. Latinos are socialized to a close connection with family. The pillar of the Latino culture is the family. For Latinos, family includes not only immediate family but also extended family, including grandparents, aunts, uncles, cousins (Rodriguez), and godparents. If you have been introduced to the family, you know that you have succeeded in making a true friend in the Latino culture.

Family ties and loyalty are highly esteemed. Young adults live at home with parents or family until they marry. Adult children help their parents financially and often the elderly live with either the eldest child or the daughter. Latinos rarely consider the idea of placing their elderly in assisted living or a nursing home. This is why, for the most part, one who reaches the head of the household has a great probability of winning the entire family. Latinos value close relationships, cohesiveness, and cooperativeness with family members. Family does not necessarily mean blood relation; relationships are developed through both immediate and extended family members: madrina (godmother), padrino (godfather), as well as close friends of the family (Marin & Triandis, 1985).

The Value of El Respeto

Respeto (respect) implies submission to authority in a hierarchical relationship. Respeto emphasizes the importance of framing clear boundaries and knowing one's place. Parents, the elderly, and authorities, according to Latino cultural values, have earned the right to respeto. The eldest female, *Mama,* is the Matriarch and she is the watchdog over her children's homes. *Papa* (the eldest male) is the Patriarch and all the men of the family go to him for guidance and the final word. *Respeto* also applies to the way the wife honors the man of the house by being submissive. Respeto can be translated into the professional relationship, causing individuals not to express disagreement even when they do not see eye-to-eye with their leader (Santiago-Rivera et al., 2002). Respect, trust, and loyalty all stem from familismo. Latino-Americans are members of a culture whose values are strong about the concept of family— familismo—the strong family ties and loyalty, and the collective nature or collectivismo (González & Benitez, 2010).

The Value of El Collectivismo

Latinos are a known to be collective society, as stated in Chapter 2. Researchers believe that from a cultural psychological perspective, collectivism is the construct that summarizes the fundamental difference in how the relationship between individuals and societies is interpreted (Oyerman & Lee, 2008). Collectivism emphasizes the interdependence of every member in that society or group. That cultural element is the polar opposite of individualism.

Collectivism stresses the importance and priority of group goals over personal goals. The Latino culture is collective in nature; therefore, the members have difficulty making decisions based on personal gain. Corona indicates that because Latinos are a collectivist culture they value relationships over personal needs. Research has supportive evidence that Hispanics emphasize that the building of emotional bonds (*confianza*) increases camaraderie and cooperation (Bordas, 1999). Because the Latino culture is such a familismo (family-oriented) and collectivismo (collectivist) culture by training, when you have empowered even a small segment, you have empowered the entire group. The Latino culture has maintained its cultural values of collectivism because people have suffered biases throughout their lives. Included in collectivism are *la simpatia* and *el personalismo*. These two are essential in both familismo and in collectivismo (Benitez & Gonzalez).

The Value of La Simpatia and El Personalismo

La simpatia (loving kindness) is a value framed with an emphasis on being polite and pleasant. This value is taught in one's formative years. You must be simpatico/a despite stress and adversity. Avoiding hostility and confrontation is a key part of simpatia. As a result, most Latinos are not comfortable openly expressing disagreement or displeasure (Rodriguez).

Interpersonal relationships are extremely important to Latinos they encourage developing warm and friendly relationships. This Latinos name *Personalismo*. Latinos more easily develop these relationships with other Latinos since through the cultural they are naturally formed. These relationships are informal, embracing and cheerful as opposed to impersonal and overly formal relationships (Santiago-Rivera et al., 2002).

The Value of Time

Another stereotype of Latinos is that they are disorganized and insensitive to timeframes. For the Latino, time is a precious commodity that should be savored and that the focus should be on the here and now (Rodriguez). The Latin American is monochromic, a culture with no adherence to time schedules (Hall, 1973). The value of time for the Latino is placed on family and attention to people rather than schedules. People take precedence to appointments, work and time sensitivity. Time, Latino style, should be enjoyed and not rushed. Time encompasses a broader perspective than just a clock or a schedule; it has to do with how Latinos view their destinies because time is strongly connected to their spirituality. Some believe that destiny and one's path is controlled by God (Rodriguez).

It may be suggested that Latin Americans do not view the future, or plan for the future, in the same way the Western world would. In a study done by the Pew Hispanic Center (PHC), forty-two percent of Latinos believe that there is no point to plan for the future because nobody controls it (Pew Hispanic Center, 2002). Appointments are scheduled with a ballpark time mentality (Katz 2006). Culturally, family comes first. The Latin American's priorities differ significantly from the Western world.

In examining the psychology of time and time perspective, PHC recognized that the centrality of time perspective in many domains of psychology is important. Time perception is psychological, and since culture plays such a significant role in our psyche, it is important to understand how other cultures deal with time (Zimbardo & Boyd). It is important to understand that different cultures value time differently, neither better nor worse. They place their value on different things relative to time. While some value success that is determined by work and financial stability, others value family, people, and enjoying life one moment at a time. All value time but focus their attention differently.

Latin American Core Beliefs, Values & Ethics

There are distinctive behaviors of a people or a culture that make sense only when seen through the basic beliefs, assumptions, and values of that group. The US is composed of diverse ethnic groups and cultures that have helped shape American values. Nevertheless, some individuals and groups have their own sets of values that are particularly different from those of mainstream U.S. (Beane). Robert Kohls, of The Washington International Center reports

"We are a nation of communities... a brilliant diversity spread like stars, like a thousand points of light in a broad and peaceful sky.

George H. W. Bush

that Americans think of themselves as varied and unpredictable. They believe they are only slightly influenced by family, church, or school. And they believe they personally chose which values they want to espouse.

There is a list of common values that would fit Americans perfectly. This list of typical American values sharply contrasts to the values commonly held by people of other countries (Kohls). The list follows:

- *Change*—change is linked to development, improvement, progress, and growth; they believe in the virtue of hard work and that each individual has a responsibility to do his or her best (Kohls). In comparison, Latinos also believe in hard work and the responsibility to work hard for the family—this falls under the familismo Latino value.

- *Time and Its Control*—time is very important to Americans; getting things accomplished on time is valued over developing deep interpersonal relations. Schedules are meant to be planned and kept at the smallest detail. Americans value guarding time, using it wisely, setting and working toward a goal, expending time today that will yield fruits of our labor to be enjoyed later (Kohls). In contrast, Latinos are a monochromic society; they believe that time is on their side and they value people and relationships over schedules and timeframes.

- **_Individual and Privacy_**—Americans are individualistic in their thoughts and actions; they believe they are just a little different, a little unique, a little more special than other members of the same group; individualism means a greater variety of opinions and the freedom to express them anywhere and at any time. Privacy is perceived by Americans as necessary, desirable and satisfying for all humans. In contrast, Latinos are a collective society. They are always considerate of others and make decisions that are in the best interest of the family or group (Kohls). In contrast Latinos are a very collective society, there is very little privacy everyone in the family knows everyone's business. Privacy is considered distance and possibly disrespectful. Familismo and collectivismo negate individualism and privacy.

- **_Competition and Free Enterprise_**—Americans believe that competition brings out the best in people; it challenges and/or forces people to produce their best. Because they value competition, Americans have created an economic system to go with it—free enterprise (Kohls). In comparison, Latinos are very competitive in sports games such as futbol (soccer) or baseball they compete hard; however, in business it depends on region and family system. Cubans and Central Americans are far more competitive than other Latino regions. Competitiveness also depends on family values.

- *Future Orientation*—nearly all Anglo focus is directed toward realizing that there is a better future, devaluing the past and at times even the present. They do not enjoy the present because they are in constant preparation for the future. Even in the best of conditions, they are always preparing for a later-and-greater event that will culminate in something more worthwhile (Kohls). In contrast, Latinos make tentative plans for the future—making long-term plans and devaluing the past. Not being appreciative of the present is considered "falta de respeto" (ungrateful—disrespectful) to God. Even when stating plans for the future Latinos always conclude with the phrase "si Dios quiere" (if God willing).

- *Action/Work Orientation*—Americans have a "don't just stand there" value system. People should always take action; action—any action is preferable to inaction. The idea of relaxation is frowned upon. Relaxation time is limited, preplanned, and focused on rejuvenating their ability to work harder and more productively. Leisure activities should assume a relatively small portion of a person's life. Americans have a no-nonsense attitude toward life, creating people who are addicted to their work, who are frustrated when they are kept away from their work, even during evening hours and weekends. This has endearingly been coined "workaholic" (Kohls). In contrast, Latinos love life. They live it to the fullest; they believe in relaxation and they enjoy family, friends and community whenever possible. Latinos have a life balanced with work and play. The personalismo value comes to play here in that take time to develop relationships.

- *Informality*—the American society is extremely informal, to the degree that people may be disrespectful to those in authority. Leaders ask to be called by their first names and not by title (Mr., Mrs., Ms. etc.). Informal attire in places such as theater and symphony is common. Greetings are also an informal "hi" to anyone, from a person in authority to a best friend (Kohls). In contrast, Latinos highly value "el respeto," that plays out in every area they address—the elderly, parents, and authority with the highest respect. They always address people of position with the proper surname. This is the "respeto" value.

- *Directness—Openness and Honesty*—Americans are completely honest in delivering their negative evaluations. Anything but a direct approach is considered dishonest and insincere. They quickly lose confidence in and distrust anyone who is not forthcoming and direct. That kind of behavior is considered manipulative and untrustworthy (Kohls). In contrast the Latino culture is "simpatico/a" centered on being polite and pleasant. Being direct even when delivering negative information is considered rude and unpleasant.

- *Practicality and Efficiency*—Americans described themselves as extremely realistic, practical, and efficient. Important decisions are made based on practical considerations. They pride themselves in not being philosophical or theoretically oriented. Pragmatism is very important; they belittle "emotional" and "subjective" evaluations in favor of "rational" and "objective" assessments (Kohls). In contrast, because of religious (la iglesia) beliefs, Latinos believe in fate, important decisions are discussed and evaluated by family (familismo), they are emotional (simpatia) kind and generous, and subjective (personalismo) caring about others.

- *Materialsim/Acquisitiveness*—Americans are very materialistic; they like to believe that acquiring things is a result of hard work and serious intent—a reward; they value and collect more objects than most people of the world would ever dream of owning, giving more priority to obtaining, maintaining, and protecting their objects than they do to enjoying interpersonal relationships (Kohls). In contrast, since for the most part Latinos have been an indigenous population, material objects have never been the core of their interest; they find much more value in: familismo, collectivismo, simpatia, personalismo, and conciencia. Overall, people are at the heart of Latinos.

The Anglo culture originated predominantly in Protestant Northern Europe with minimal or nonexistent Native American influence. The Hispanic culture was born in Southern Europe with heavy Catholic Christian influence, then later crossed with a strong influence from Native America, with a lesser but significant element of African culture. These influences have birthed yet a newer kind of Latino.

The comparisons are made to show the commonalities and the differences that have the potential of creating a great collaboration. As we have discussed Latinos, are saturated in cultural values, many that were formed from strong religious beliefs. Family is their lifeline and they are a collective society. Latinos in the US, for the most part, have lived in two cultures, and often in two opposing sets of values. Becoming acculturated and assimilated has been a struggle in both their Latino circles. The result is that they believe they have forgotten who they are and in the US culture; some believe they have outdated beliefs. The Hispanic culture has been shaped for more than half a millennia by a unique set of historical circumstances. Such comparisons were made specifically because these values and morals equate ethical practices that are a perquisite for great business leadership.

> *"Preservation of one's own culture does not require contempt or disrespect for other cultures."*
>
> Cesar Chavez

Compare and Contrast Latino Versus U.S. Values and Ethics

As stated previously, Latino values and ethics are often at the polar opposite from the US cultural values. We will explore how Latin Americans and North Americans differ so vastly in core beliefs, values, and ethics. One set of cultural values is not better than others; we want to explain the differences.

"What we have to do . . . is to find a way to celebrate our diversity and debate our differences without fracturing our communities."

Hillary Clinton

Let's begin with how each is culturally socialized. There are two cultural social groups: collective and individualist. The collective society is interdependent. They view the self as part of a larger social network that includes family, coworkers, community, and others to whom they are socially connected. Individualists have an independent view of self as an entity that is explicit, autonomous, self-contained, and endowed with a unique propensity (Hofstede, 1991; Markus & Kitayama, 1991).

Compare and Contrast

Latin Americans/Non-Westerners	Americans & European
Others focused	Ego focused
Promote social harmony	Jealousy
Indebted to someone (others)	Pride
Connected to someone (others)	Self autonomous entity
Familiarity to someone (others)	Heterogeneous –
Simple society	Loose, aloof,
Same	Permissive of
Language	individual
Religion	expression
Social customs	Complex society
	Affluent society

The stark difference between Latin American and Western American core beliefs, values, and ethics is demonstrated in different reactions and actions by the Latino and the American. Almost from the onset, you will notice that Latinos are expressive, demonstrative, and portray very deep emotions whether happy or sad. Because Latinos are a collective society, taking care of their own is part of their core belief; a self-imposed obligation to share the possessions, food and often wealth. You will often find that Latino businesses are family run. A Latino's sense of family and community derives from their social nature and multigenerational living (Benitez). Latino leaders are different in their core values and ethics. The need and desire to be in leadership roles differs from Caucasians, in that the pursuit is to use one's skill for the well-being of the family, kin, and community and not solely for personal gain. The appetite to reach middle-class status is the dedication to reach such success for the benefit of others in the family and/or community. Leadership status will be determined by the character of Latinos passionately committed to a new wealth and quality that establishes new forms of justice and compassion that allows all to share and prosper. In the Latino culture, a professional is someone who professes values of truth, justice, love, wisdom—someone who stands passionately for life (Abalos, 2007). If this is true, you will also find that as Latinos acculturate and assimilate (mostly the second and third generations) their cultural value systems change.

The New Latino-Americano

As we have discussed Latino core beliefs, values and ethics notably differ from US cultural values. But there is yet another group—the New Latino-Americans, the second- and third-generation Latinos. This extraction of Latino lives between social cultural beliefs, values, and ethical norms. Although many Latino cultural values are ingrained from birth, the more assimilated Latinos succumb to the American cultural values, developing a hybrid of cultures, often moving further away from their cultural core values. Latinos who are more acculturated to mainstream American culture may stray from some of these values, but never without the continuous reminders from family and kin. Given the Latino multigenerational population, the acculturation process has developed intrafamilial value differences, often at the expense of varying their endorsements of Latino values (Smokowski, Rose, & Bacallao, 2008; Szapocznik, Kurtines, & Fernandez, 1980; Szapocznik, Kurtines, Foote, Pérez-Vidal, & Hervis, 1986).

Second-generation Latino-Americans, the twenty million adult US-born children of immigrants, are substantially better off than the immigrants themselves on key measures of socioeconomic attainment. Their incomes are higher; there are more college graduates and homeowners; few live in poverty (Pew Research Center, 2013). The children of Latino immigrants come closer to achieving the "American Dream" than their parents (Taylor). The second generation is more likely to speak English fluently, to have friends and spouses outside their ethnic or racial group, and to think of themselves as "typical American" (Pew Research Center). The second generation is doing considerably better financially at a much more rapid rate (Taylor). But this, many Latinos may say, is at the expense of losing many of their cultural values. Those Latinos who adopt this cultural hybrid live two cultural norms: one at home (Latino cultural values) and another in their professional/academic life (the US cultural value system).

The Relationship between Core Beliefs, Values, and Ethics to Worldview

Core beliefs, values, and ethical standards codify worldview. Worldviews are formulated on some faith-based understanding of the universe—be it examined or unexamined, implicit or explicit, simplistic or sophisticated—it is your worldview. Once developed, one's worldview accounts for one's core beliefs, values, and ethical standards—and decisions made, treatment of others, and how you conduct yourself. Somehow, through our worldview, we develop functional assumptions that help sort through and make sense from our experiences. Each individual's worldview always has a faith-based component—even nonreligious individuals have faith in something (Gousmett, 1996).

A Cultural Worldview

The infrastructure for one's worldview begins to be developed at birth from family, faith, environment, and academic status. This is the conglomeration of experiences that configure culture. Cultures are complex and derivative of environment, upbringing, and an accumulation of experiences. Worldview is then perceived from this "norm." Anthropologists have long believed that culture stands for a way of life of a group of people. The sum of their learned behaviors, attitudes, moral and ethical values, and religious beliefs are all formulated through culture. One's worldview is birthed from culture.

A Faith Based Worldview

The Christian worldview provides an interpretive framework that solidly supports and informs commonly held social values such as the inherent value of each individual despite personal characteristics, self-determination, and personally responsible freedom of choice, and responsibility for the common good, including help for the poor and oppressed. The Christian worldview will also challenge other values and theories, such as "might makes right," the exploitation of the weak by the strong, and extreme moral relativism. Conversely, other worldviews, including materialism, empiricism, and postmodern subjectivism will lead to quite contrasting conclusions regarding these values (Sherwood).

The Impact Values and Ethics Have on Latino Leadership

Thus far, we have established what values, morals, and ethics are and what the Latino value system is. Now let's explore how their value system influences their leadership. The *Latino Leadership Competency Model* study was created by Gonzalez and Benitez to gain a better understanding of the behavioral patterns that affect the Latinos' successful personal and professional lives. The findings were as follows: there are four types of emerging Latino leaders:

➢10 percent opted for a more cautious style;

➢18 percent a more competitive style,

➢24 percent a more social manner

➢and the majority, 45 percent, were of a more caring persuasion.

The variations in leadership styles were dominated by immigration generation. Those who rendered a *cautious* leadership style (ten percent) were foreign-born and a few second generation. These leaders remained attached to their country-of-origin and its traditions, yet they were bicultural and bilingual. They had a propensity to be more humble, sincere, and sensitive to those they lead. Those of the *competitive* leadership style were largely second- and third-generation Latinos. Their perception of themselves was American; they were well educated, English-dominant, with basic Spanish skills; they were assimilated into the mainstream American culture. These Latino leaders were optimistic, determined, and focused on delivering results; they covered all the bases and did everything necessary to ensure success. They exhibited high levels of competence and professional knowledge and had difficulty asking for help. These leaders preferred fast-paced work environments in which they can stay active, grow, and continually learn (Gonzalez & Benitez, 2010).

Then those who were had more of a *sociable* leadership style, the twenty-four percent, were amid the most acculturated second- and third-generation Latino leaders. These leaders had basic Spanish speaking skills, were resourceful, flexible, and creative. They are not afraid to offer ideas, inspiration, and possibilities. These leaders are enthusiastic team players; their strengths are in persuasion rather than competition. They are confident, fashionable, and fun. The sociable Latino leader wants recognition, flexibility, and interaction. Lastly, the larger sample (forty-five percent) was the *caring* leadership style of Latino leader and was from the first generation. These leaders displayed strong spiritual and moral foundations, tended to be relaxed, open, patient, and approachable. Their trademark is hard work, trustworthiness, and integrity. Their core values are founded in keeping their word even if it entails sacrifice. These leaders focus on values, fairness, equality, and impartiality to maintain harmonious relationships. Lastly, these findings resolved that although there was a dominant leadership style for most of these Latino leaders, many interchanged leadership styles within this index (Gonzalez & Benitez, 2010).

How Core Beliefs Shape Latino Businesses

Assimilation and acculturation to the U.S. value system is almost nonexistent in Latino-owned business. For most Latino business owners, because we are the sum of our experiences, the way a leader leads is largely attached to core beliefs, values, and ethics. This is greatly evident in Latino business.

One of the early games we learn to play as children is "follow the leader." The object of the game is to do as the leader does; the leader sets the tone for occurs.

Fast forward to adulthood and leaders continue to have the same effect on followers. Values and ethics govern the core in which individuals operate. Leaders have their sets of beliefs, values and codes of ethics.

Malphurs asserts that, "As the leader goes, so goes the organization" and at its core, this is the reason why (Malphurs). You will find that when you understand the culture of a company and the company's values and ethical practices, there is a direct relation to the leader(s).

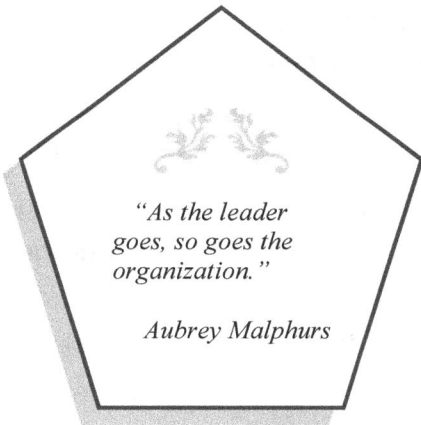

"As the leader goes, so goes the organization."

Aubrey Malphurs

For the most part, Latinos have a very strong code of values and ethics. They are risk takers, independent, prioritize family above all else, have a strong work ethic, ambitious, are self-believing, religious, and have a deep pride in heritage (Loretta Marketing Group). Values determine how things "should be done" through the communication of purpose and values. A cohort colleague argues that core values are formed from a personal worldview and leaders influence their organizations based on who they are as individuals (Sweeny, 2011). Core values determine leadership style and organizations are run on leader values; these are firmly welded.

The one thing that Latinos hold near and dear is their Spanish language. The fourth largest Spanish-speaking population resides in the United States. Bilingualism is an advantage in personal and professional growth, in social encounters, and in an educational environment. According to Synovate's 2010 US Market Diversity Market Report, at a national level, fifty-five percent of Latino adults speak Spanish at home, or they speak Spanish more often than English, twenty-three percent speak English at home, and twenty-two percent speak Spanish and English equally or are bilingual. But the report does not provide insights into the capability of speaking either language at home. Numerous organizations discourage Latinos from speaking Spanish at work, not realizing having Spanish speakers on staff can facilitate the connection between their clients and their products or services. Since Spanish is the second most spoken language in the world at 347 million (Wikipedia). Many domestic companies place great value on their Spanish speaking bilingual staff offering them monetary compensation for their proficiency.

Companies are created from the ideas, thoughts, and core beliefs of the leader. In other words, to separate an individual's core values from the way they run and create policies and procedures is impossible. What the leader believes at the core will mold the way the organization is run from beginning to end. Morally sensitive leaders are the essential feature of any good organization. The ethical value system of the leadership will be displayed throughout that organization beginning with its mission and vision. The mission defines the organization's primary objectives and the vision portrays the ethical mindset of the leadership (Ciulla, 2004).

We began this series by explaining who the Latino is and we moved to leadership styles. Servant leadership, we explained, is the essence of positively transforming followers/employees. Servant leadership is a direct con-sequence of employee satisfaction, increased productivity, belief in leadership, and company loyalty (Winston, 2002). This induces creativity and revenue increase.

In this segment, we learned that an *Individualist* society is egocentric and a *Collectivist* society is others-focused. One is a servant leadership style; the opposing leadership style is egocentric. Ego is the invisible line item on every company's profit-and-loss statement; unseen but not unfelt. Ego diminishes the honesty of what is communicated in a meeting, which lowers trust, diminishes sincerity with which people listen, clouds the accuracy of assessment, and alters the openness of debates. Ego is the determining factor that decides whether a team is held back by performance that's "good enough" or breaks through that barrier to achieve greatness (Marcum & Smith, 2007). Leaders with big egos create hostile environments and are a danger to their companies. This person can run a company to the ground. The way to assess the direction of the company is to know the core values of its leader. Leaders, be aware, because your thumbprint is all over your company and the company will always be reflective of your values and ethics.

Although painting Latinos with a broad brush by stating that all Latinos are "servant leaders" is an absolute that cannot be supported, we can comfortably state that collectivism has a propensity to birth servant leadership, because Latino leaders notoriously place greater emphasis on family and community than on the individual. Latino leaders also have strong work ethics and want to provide for and protect their families. Latinos perceive their responsibilities as a badge of honor and proactively seek opportunities to contribute in a respectful and honorable way at home, at work, and in the community. Latino leaders highly value spirituality, compassion, caring, and respect (Gonzalez & Benitez). This approach is comparable to two schools of thought—Greenleaf's servant leadership and Covey's new leadership paradigms. Covey attests that the leader of the future is one who creates a culture or value system based on the principles of service, integrity, fairness, and equity (Covey, 2004).

"Ego is our silent partner – too often with controlling interest."
Cullen Hightower

Only in the good and the right can there be reflective stability. The right inevitably conflicts with the good and influences its adjustment (Joas, 2000). Great leaders are typically connected to a cause related to their professional spheres. They also tap into the deep convictions of others and connect those feelings to the purpose of the organization. They show the meaning of people's everyday work to that larger purpose (Kotter, 1998). Every organization has its personal value and ethics DNA; it is directly linked to the leadership.

Lassoing it All Together: El Latino as Patrón, Jefe ó Boss (Owner, Leader, or Supervisor)

Review the essential components. We began by defining values, morals, and ethics. We then unfolded the core cultural values of the Latino. We analyzed the relationship between core beliefs, values, and ethics of varying worldviews, compared and contrasted values and ethics of Latin Americans/Non Westerners vs. American & Europeans, and lastly we examined how core beliefs, values, and ethics influence Latino businesses.

The Pew Research Hispanic Center documented that between 2000 and 2010, a forty-seven percent increase of new businesses launched were by Latino business-owners. These numbers are will increase and this is exciting news for Latinos who historically have been lagging behind mainstream America. The data proves that Latinos are building their confidence and are stepping up to leadership roles. There are many more Hispanics finishing high school and continuing on to higher education, and they are succeeding in business.

The rich culture and strong values of the Latino plus technological globalization makes Latinos the primary candidates for business leadership. But when talking about Latinos as business leaders, what makes them most appealing is that they are rich in diversity; this is essential when operating globally. The Latino's cultural values, such as respeto (respect), simpatia (warmth and friendliness), personalismo (building relationships) plus their bilingual proficiency is positioning Latinos to be the obvious business leader. The values, morals, and business ethics that Latinos possess are precisely what is necessary for 21st Century globalization, and Latinos are prepared.

Daniel Goleman proposes that emotional intelligence, empathy, and cross-cultural sensitivity are key components for effective leadership. By default, due to the increase in Latino population in the not-too-distant future, Latinos will become the role models in leadership (Gonzalez & Bennitez). Latinos will complement and challenge perceptions and practices in the mainstream and in corporate America (Llopis, 2013). Nothing can guarantee that future generations will hold on to the Latino heritage, culture, and identities. It is all contingent upon the encouragement Latino leaders receive from mainstream organizations to support them in retaining, developing, and advancing (Gonzalez & Benitez). There will also need to be more support from the Latino community in developing Latino leadership.

Chapter 4

Global Drivers of Change That Realign Latino Positioning

There are global drivers that transition one era to the next. History proved this repeatedly; there was the Stone Age, the Agricultural Age, the Industrial Age, and now the Information Age.

Technology has positioned change drivers on steroids. Never in the history of the world has there been such rapid changes than throughout the 21st Century, change so rapid that things are outdated the moment they hit the mainstream. These changes affect every area of our lives, especially our society.

> *"Change does not roll in on the wheels of inevitability, but comes through continuous struggle"*
>
> *MLK, Jr.*

Social change occurs in the macro world and not in the quantum physics; it is a cycle of changing seasons, life, and death (Bishop & Hines). Social change involves so many components such as *ideology*, the belief system that defines social and political arrangements and relations that develop in long-term work environments. There is the *competition* component created by scarcity of employment, causing people to compete for positions, and for maintaining their employment; and *polity*, the process of deciding who gets what, when, and how. Additionally, there is the *economy,* because economic forces shape and guide lives. These are all part of a continual cycle. Marx suggests that the way people obtain their livelihood also establishes their social institutions. Finally, "forced changes" also affect structural strains because it upsets the equilibrium of the social system; these are change-producing strains (Vago).

This chapter will cover the external drivers of change that constructively affected the Latino in the United States. As said previously, the Latino community grew four percent between 2000 and 2010, and the prediction is that they will continue growing at a much more rapid rate than any other group in the United States for the coming decades, reaching 22 million by 2020 and about 108 million by 2040 (Cartagena, 2005). This shift has restructured the positioning of Hispanics in extraordinary ways. The population growth emerging with the global need for people who are multilingual and multicultural will make the Latinos the most logical choice for leadership roles. To understand best the impact the Hispanic population will have on United States communities and businesses, we will evaluate the essence of that population and how the shift will alter the Latino-American.

We will analyze this change through the eyes of Kurt Lewin's "Force Field Analysis," which helps visualize the opposing forces inherent in any issue or situation. By analyzing the driving forces (those that stimulate change) and the restraining forces (those that resist change), one has a wider prospective to determine an action plan. Conversely, you can then use your analysis to think about how to strengthen the forces that support the change and weaken the opposing forces. This will ensure that the change is successful (MindTools.com). Another instrument we will look at is the STEEP analysis, which analyzes the various external factors affecting Latino business or organizations. The STEEP model looks at the Social, Technological, Economic, Environmental, and Political implications. We will address the effect of these external changes on Latino business leaders. In this chapter, we will draw a panoramic view that will allow us to understand the trends in social change that are repositioning the Latino.

Quick Overview and Amalgamation

As specified in Chapter 1, there has been an increase in the Latino population. There has also been a significant decrease in undocumented Latino immigrants. The projections suggest that this minority group will be ninety-plus million by 2050 and will account for at least twenty-nine plus percent of the United States (Pew Research: Social & Demographic Trends). Then the Latino will no longer be a minority. This chapter also addressed the increase in Latino business owners and the projections for an even larger increase in Hispanic business leaders. The trend of Latinos affecting every aspect of the national and international landscape becomes more obvious than ever. Domestically, Latinos are progressively sewn into the fabric of popular culture, the food, the music, the workforce, consumerism, politics, and the American national identity. Then, as referenced in Chapter 2, the status of Latino Emotional Intelligence makes the Latino business owner prepared for leadership roles. Chapter 3, about the Latino's values, morals, and ethics also proves that Latinos are capable of communicating both domestically and internationally because they have the skills to interact socially. They also have much agapáo love; typically doing the right thing for the right reason. Having agapáo plus high levels of integrity help Latinos with the interaction necessary in these volatile times. The Latinos' values and ethics postures them for the shift in social change.

The Significance of This New Social Change to Latinos

It has been reiterated repeatedly that today change is coming at a much more rapid pace than ever. These changes are taking our nation by storm. Approaching 2050 will mean

> *"No real social change has ever been brought about without a revolution...revolution is but a thought carried into action."*
>
> *Emma Goldman*

unprecedented diversity never seen in the history of our nation;

the driving force of this change will be Latinos. Demographers report that there will be no racial or ethnic majority among the general population in the United States and that the Latino population will double. Conversely, the role of Latinos is significantly reshaping both the political and the economic climate of our nation.

As reported earlier, the Hispanic population is rapidly increasing in this country. Therefore, the challenges this community faces must be addressed now. The disparities faced by the Latino community in health care, education, and economic indicators can no longer be ignored. Local and national leaders must develop policies that will address these disparities (Cárdenas and Kerby, 2012).

The Arm Twist to Assimilate

"One nation under God, with liberty and justice for all"—these words from the Pledge of Allegiance, allege freedom. "Freedom" is a word typically synonymous with the United States and the reason that for hundreds of years immigrants have come to America, seeking this freedom. For Latinos, the greatest conflict has been the strong pressure to assimilate and acculturate by turning their backs on their culture. This struggle is most monumental for the many Latinos who resist neglecting their roots. These Latinos have battled with overt rejection by mainstream America, characterized as non-American or immigrants (Rumbout, National Research Council, 2006).

The turmoil for too many Latinos has been their inability to merge their private world of a poverty-stricken environment and inhibited Spanish-speaking parents with their newfound public existence. This new world finds them drinking latte and eating croissants while discussing the value of medieval literature with Ivy-league colleagues (Abalos, 2007). Most do not feel the same freedom to be Latino and share the richness of that side of their world. Latinos feel fragmented—and they are; they live in two worlds that have them split and feeling disloyal in both environments.

"When a person or cultural group is cut off from its feelings, personal sources, and institutions, it is also cut off from its creative depths" (Abalos, 2007). Because Latinos love their native language, food, music, and culture does not mean they reject the American culture; it means only that they love who they are and value the exuberance of the merging of both cultures. Latinos believe in the same values as all other Americans. They work hard and cherish the opportunity to get ahead, raise their children well, and give them the best education possible. Latinos do yearn to be successful. But at their core, Latinos believe that to be successful at improving our society they must value family and the idea that we each are obliged to help those in need (Cartagena, 2013). To improve one's own quality of life, it should be for the good of society. As discussed in Chapter 3, this is one of the values of the Hispanic.

Speak English; You're in America!

I presented on the Latinization of America. As I explained the growth in the population and the repositioning of Latinos in the US, I sadly experienced this: someone in the audience openly announced, "Latinos need to assimilate and acculturate just as he did when he came from Portugal. Forget your language and your culture; just assimilate and be like everybody else." He proceeded to say, "If you can't let go of your roots, you need to return to your country of origin." And what if your country of origin is America? It would then seem that there is not far to go.

On August 28, 1995, during a child custody hearing in Amarillo, Texas, State District Attorney Samuel Kiser ordered Martha Laureano, a US citizen of Mexican descent, to speak only English at home to her daughter. He said that she was abusing the child and relegating her to the position of a housemaid. When this hit the media, it rocked Latino households around the country and sparked an outcry from community leaders. The judge only echoed what many Anglo-Americans have believed for years.

Hispanics have always been at odds with white and black English-speaking Americans about language. Those who support the constitutional amendment that makes English the official language fear that the rising number of immigrants, especially the flood of Latin Americans during the past few decades, will Balkanize the nation's linguistic groups to make

English speakers strangers in their land (Gonzalez, 2011). According to <u>2010 Hispanic American Census Facts</u>, there are currently 37 million residents in the U.S. who speak Spanish at home. And more than half of these Spanish speakers also speak English very well.

Sadly, despite their efforts to assimilate, Latinos continue to suffer overt criticism for who they are. The two most recent cases of lashing were Mexican-American Sebastien De La Cruz and Mark Anthony a Puerto Rican-American. Both men sang in the American public—De La Cruz sang the national anthem in June, 2013 in San Antonio, Texas (<u>Huffington Post</u>). A month later, Anthony sang "God Bless America." Both were judged non-American and openly attacked for singing these American anthems. Both are American. In a world that is rapidly consolidating, how can the merging cultures understand, love, and respect others without losing themselves in the process?

The concern for many is the way that Latinos are repeatedly discriminated against. There are repetitive court cases of discrimination against Spanish speakers, even when they are specifically hired to communicate in Spanish with Spanish-speaking customers. Given the conflicts between these lower court decisions and the spread of English-only laws at the state level, the Supreme Court will eventually be forced to tackle language discrimination (Gonzalez, 2011). The longstanding battles over civil rights and racial equality are now taking a new direction, promising to reshape race relations and common notions of a "minority." New census projections report that Whites will be the new minority by 2043 and Hispanics will reshape the nation's schools, workforce, and electorate redefining this long-held notion of race (Yen, Latino Politics, 2012).

Education Attainment

The Problem

The school system, for hundreds of years, has been the battleground for assimilation. Millions of Germans, Italians, Poles, Jews, Greeks, and others have been transformed into English- speakers in the quest to assimilate. However, today the same school system is an agent of social change. Although they have altered their tactics to avoid assimilation of Hispanic children, including efforts to maintain and strengthen their ethnic identities, they do teach them in their native language and inculcate their native culture. This process has had an adverse effect and has served only to segregate Hispanic children keeping them from their English-speaking peers, even after they have acquired basic English skills (Chavez, 1991).

It is no secret—Latinos have been known to be the least-educated ethnic group. The educational experience for Hispanics has been one of accumulated disadvantage. Most begin formalized education without economic and social resources and for the most part, schools are ill equipped to compensate for these disparities. The initial disadvantage often stems from having immigrant parents who lack knowledge of the US education system and socioeconomic status. Latinos have the lowest rates of high school and college degree attainment, not because they do not appreciate the need for an education and obtaining stable and meaningful work, but largely because of socioeconomic status (Abalos, 2007).

In part, the underlying issue may be that many families remain cloistered in Spanish-speaking neighborhoods. Their strong work ethic may compound the problem by driving their children into the workforce before they complete high school (Cartagena). There is the assumption that affirmative action has positioned Latinos with the benefit of achieving higher education, yet it is quite contrary. The problem is that this does not change the representation of Latinos in higher education. Actually, the pool of Hispanic applicants to college is substantially smaller than the representation of this group in the population. Also since many Hispanics have a greater likelihood of coming from inadequate high schools, many of their test scores and preparation are lower than for whites on average (McArdle, 2013). The difficulty of extracting affirmative action serves only to undermine the educational, economic, and political gains of Latinos (Chapa, Latinos Remaking America).

The Transmutation

The pain for the average Latino is not that there is overt hatred directed toward him or her, but it's more about being invisible, neglected, and considered unimportant. Nevertheless,

Hispanics are on an upward ascension toward success. In the past decade, the number of Hispanics graduating from college with Associate or Bachelor's degrees has had a sevenfold increase, outpacing other groups. Not only has the number of Hispanic degrees increased but also has the Latinos' share of college degree recipients. The number of degrees conferred in 2010 for Latinos of all ages has reached record levels; this was confirmed by the US Department of Education's Nation Center for Education Statistics. They reported that 140,000 Bachelor's degrees and 112,000 Associate degrees were awarded to Hispanics—these numbers are at an all-time high. Although Latinos continue to lag behind other groups, these numbers prove a positive incline (Pew Research Hispanic Center, 2012). The Huffington Post asserts that the high school dropout rate decreased between years 2000 to 2011 for Latinos aged 16-24. And in 2012, sixty-nine percent of Latino high school graduates moved directly from high school to college, two points higher than their white counterparts. Yet, there is so much more that Latino graduates can achieve if given the holistic approach (Agilera, 2013).

The Supreme Court determined in 1982 that educators did not have the right to ask the citizenship status of students enrolling in schools. The ability to attend school was an opportunity provided to students, despite how they enter the school doors; everyone deserves the best education available. The law is commonly known as the "No Child Left Behind" act (NCLB). The premise is that when our nation's immigrants prosper, our country prospers. This act ensures that school districts are held accountable for student, including special populations. And that, despite race, zip code, language, ability, or country of origin, it's always best to graduate students equipped with the skills necessary to benefit society. Since the NCLB enactment, students are no longer routinely marginalized and hidden. There is evidence of academic improvement among immigrant children and graduations rates are on a steady incline. The achievement gap between minority and non-minority students is decreasing (Briggs, Bush Center, 2013).

Even this slight increase in Latinos earning higher education degrees has begun the transposition of Latinos into middle-class status. Although Latinos have, for the most part, resided in five primary states: California, Texas, Florida, New York, and Illinois. Today they are migrating to states such as South Carolina, Kentucky, Arkansas, Minnesota, and North Carolina (Pew Hispanic Center, 2011). As they migrate into the mainstream, they are moving to geographical areas where the economy is doing well (Koebler, US News, 2011). Many have been absorbed by the mainstream and have become invisible in plain sight (Chavez). This movement is the perfect storm and will be just the jolt the economy needs.

Business-ownership

The unassailable fact remains that Latino-owned businesses in the US are growing at an extraordinary rate. This trend has been sustained for at least the last decade and has grown at more than twice the national average. This has manifested itself both in the increased number and size of Latino-owned businesses (Gomez, Forbes – 2011). The Census Bureau reports that Latino revenue jumped by a staggering fifty-five percent to almost $350 million (LatinoStories.com).

> *"The Latinos continue to occupy a marginal position in society, even when they are joining the ranks of the mainstream culture."*
>
> *Arlene Davila*

Much of the research singles out Mexican-Americans, as they are the majority at 65% of the Hispanic population. For many years, Mexican-Americans have grown up in low socioeconomic means but that has changed for many. There is now an increase in those whose childhoods are cloaked in middle-class privilege. The parental pathway to middle-class status varies by generation; but many of the second generation, raised in middle-class households with low levels of education, could move to middle-class status through business ownership. And the third generation children raised in these households are much more likely to have parents with college degrees and professional occupations. Thus, they have replicated or increased beyond the class status of their parents. The one thing that has been proved is that those raised in middle-class households reap benefits that follow closely those having parents with stable middle-class incomes and as a result develop more financial resources. These benefits include middle-class neighborhoods and high-quality education, which provide richness in middle-class cultural capital (Vallejo, 2012).

This extraordinary increase solidified the first Hispanic Business Leaders' Forum on May 29, 2013. The focus of this forum was to focus on jobs, the economy, problems affecting American business, and the effective collaboration that fosters economic competitiveness in Latino communities. They gathered eighty top Hispanic business leaders from a range of industries, many from <u>Fortune 500</u> and top professional firms, the next generation of high-growth entrepreneurs, according to (Whitehouse.Gov).

STEEP

Five areas directly affect businesses, and Latino-owned businesses are no exception. As we have seen, understanding the **social** environment is crucial to business—are you selling something relevant? Latinos are in an excellent social position to sell almost anything because of their bilingual and bicultural skills. Technology is another thing businesses need to analyze. **Technology** puts the average Latino at an advantage to interact globally with anyone in the world and since Spanish is the second-most spoken language in the world, because technology brings the world closer, business can be conducted with ease. **Environment**—globalization has prepared the environment for these upscale Hispanics. It is said that Latinos will save American corporations through their ability to interact multiculturally and multilingually. Latino businesses have created a stir in the **economy** unlike before. Latino-owned businesses are having a significant impact on this recession. **Technology** is responsible for bringing the world together; this, in turn, has made globalization a fingertip away from constant availability. The STEEP method is crucial when creating Latino business.

Latinos are positioned and expected to increase their revenue contribution to the economy by eight percent annually over the next ten years, more than three times the average growth of all businesses in the US. This will give Latinos more economic influence to employ more of the population and purchase substantially more in goods and services than before. This trend has already had an impact, especially in states where there is a large population of Latinos. One thing that has always been known—small businesses are the gateway to all affluence in the US. These positive trends in Latino entrepreneurship will benefit not only the Latino community but also the entire national economy and will be instrumental in the recovery from this Great Recession (2007-2010) devastating recession (Gomez). This also supports why Latinos have a growing confidence in their personal finances (Lopez & Motel, PRHC). This explosion in the Latino economic status has a greater chance of mitigating the effects of the discrimination that Latinos have quietly suffered for many centuries. Today, Latinos by numbers and by economic status are creating an economic representation like never before (Davila, 2008).

Latino Economic Strength

Upscale Hispanic; the New Yuppie

As Latinos grow in rank, it is important to know who they really are and what they have to offer the American economy. Paulo Friere refuses to accept the stereotype of Latinos as passive or fatalistic, as if Latinos chose to be violated. He clarifies and points out that perceived fatalism is the result of particular historical and sociological conditions. The truth of the matter, he asserts, is that one group has a vested interest in making others passive so they can control them. Latinos isolate from a society and culture that insists in defining them as honorary whites, provided they "behave." This is perceived as both a personal and political act (Abalos, 2007). It is not that Latinos don't want to be American—they just do not want to be Anglo-American. And they are finding their voice and are "making it" on their terms. There is an unprecedented increase in the middle-class Latino population (Chavez) and they have been labeled "Upscale Hispanics, and considered the new yuppies."

As stated in previous chapters, there are more Latinos joining the ranks of the middle class while others have long been a part of the ranks of America's political, economic, and institutional mainstream. Unfortunately, despite this shift, Latinos continue to occupy only a marginal position in society, even as they join the ranks of mainstream culture (Davila,

2008). But this upward evolution is a rise in status, moving forward, despite opposition.

What Do Latinos Offer the Economy?

The Pew Hispanic survey report that Hispanics (33%) rate their personal finances as "excellent." Hispanics are also more optimistic, by a margin of 73% to 15%. They expect their personal financial situation and that of their family to improve over time. The Latinos have the same values and desires as do the Anglo-Americans: a better life for themselves, their children, families, and their community. The continual battle for Latinos is the pressure to assimilate; they have done so, but on their terms and without losing the integrity of their culture. This has come at a price, the disparities in household incomes. Nevertheless, Latinos are gaining ground and are changing the social and economic climate and are becoming an emerging middle-class (Chavez). According to Piston of the Latino Voice, Hispanics have become the most influential segment since the baby boomers. In 2012, they accounted for twenty-nine percent of the overall spending and expected to swell to thirty-seven percent by the end of 2013. These consumers with significant influence on the economic landscape are called "Upscale Hispanics."

These Upscale Hispanics are defined by the study as the segment of the population with annual household incomes between $50,000 and $99,999. They account for 15 million of the overall Latino population in the US and claim a median household income of about $71,000. These Latinos are regarded one of the most viable and sophisticated markets today. They are predicted to command forty percent of the Latino spending power by the end of 2013, with projections of proliferating up to 35 million by 2050 (Piston, Huffington Post, 2013).

As stated in previous chapters, Cubans' median per capita is much higher than the rest of the Hispanic population at approximately $85,000 per household. Central Americans immediately follow at $73,000 (Reimers, National Research Council). There is a notable difference in this new generation of middle-class Upscale Hispanic: they are young, family-driven and are movers and shakers (Piston, 2013).

With the astounding growth in Latino business-ownership, they have created an impressive shift to the US economy, and are taking it by storm. Many businesses are growing rapidly and are providing employment, generating more than $1 million in revenue, an increase from $29,000 five years prior (LatinoStories.com). This trend is expected to continue at least throughout this decade (US Census Bureau).

Latino Buying Power

The shift in Latino economic status has quickly drawn the eye of marketers. The "Upscale Hispanic" portion of the US consumer segment is increasing at a much faster rate than most Lamarketers previously imagined. These upscale

Hispanics reside in households with annual incomes between $50,000 and $100,000. According to the Nielson study by The Association of Hispanic Advertising Agencies, this Upscale Hispanic now totals 15 million and accounts for three out of every ten households—or twelve percent. These Upscale Hispanics represent about $500 billion of the $1.3 trillion in Hispanic consumer spending power (McClellan, Santiago Solutions Group) and are gaining ground, estimated to reach $1.5 trillion by 2015 (Llopis, 2013). In addition, the median age of Hispanics is 27.3 years (US Census 2010), making the Latino consumer nearly ten years younger than the market age of thirty-seven (Llopis) and providing the opportunity to gain even more economic strength.

The Shift in Latino Political Clout

It is no longer a secret: Latinos are gaining ground and recent elections undoubtedly proved it. For the first time in history, the 2008 and 2012 elections understood the importance of the Latino vote. As the Latino demographic expands and more of our youth are of voting age, there will be a greater share of Latino voters nationally and they will tip the scale (Hugo, PRHC). The proof is that Latinos are neither Democratic nor Republican. The problems of the Hispanic electorate are based on jobs, the economy, and education. Hispanic problems are increasingly equal to American problems and not so much immigration problems (Orchowski, USNews.com, 2011).

As Hispanic numbers increase, the importance of their political and electorate influence will also increase. In the most recent presidential elections, both parties reached out to Latinos, especially in states such as New Mexico, Arizona, Nevada, Los Angeles, Colorado, Florida, North Carolina, Wisconsin, Virginia and New York (Lopez,Taylor – Hispanic Trends Project, 2012). The presumption of these efforts is the existence of a "Latino vote," or more because Latino politics is organized to express a Latino voice in political outcomes (DeSipio). The Voting Rights Act (VRA) was granted to Latinos after 1975. Between 1975 and 1985, minorities gained voting power and Mexican-Americans in the Southwest and Puerto Ricans in New York demonstrated a new reality—Latinos exerted their power and got the attention of political candidates who had until then ignored them. Politicians suddenly became aware that by registering and campaigning to Hispanics was their newfound ability to tip the election (Gonzalez).

What has Refrained the Latino Vote?

Latinos, because of their persistence to sustain identity, culture, and language have been outcasts despite their American status. This has resulted in a "scarlet letter" type of stigma. The many years of negative external perceptions, such as public stigmatization often has a negative effect on a person's internal sense of self (Vogel, Bitman, Hammer & Wade, 2013). A stigma of any sort is a mark of shame or disgrace associated with a particular circumstance, quality, or person (Blaine, 2000).

Latino groups have experienced an overt public stigma, which implies the perception held by a group or a society that a person or group of people is socially unacceptable. That results in a self-stigma, meaning the reduction of an individual's self-esteem, thought to be because of the

internalization of negative external messages (Corrigan, 2004). This stigma has, for many years, kept Latinos from having a voice and expressing it in their electoral ballots. This has changed.

Moving Forward

Today, the Latino vote has more than quadrupled since 1976. This extraordinary increase will continue for decades, especially as Latinos begin to understand their value in the political playing field (Gonzalez). What has held Latinos back has been their immigration status, but should the process of obtaining US citizenship continue slowly, the number of Hispanics will continue to grow. Since there are more than thirty-four percent of Latinos under the age of eighteen, this large cohort of Latino youth will quickly reach voting age (Gonzalez). The time is coming and everything is aligning in support of Latinos reaching their much-deserved political influence.

Summarizing the Driving Forces of Change

The jury is "in" and the repositioning of the Latino population is on the way to achieving the long-desired American dream. To assimilate and acculturate to the American culture does not mean that Latinos must discard who they are, their traditions, culture, and language. As the numbers of Latinos grow, they will also grow in strength and will no longer believe the stigma of being less-than-others simply because they are multicultural and multilingual.

The number of Hispanics attaining high school and college degrees is increasing. With advanced educational degrees, Latinos have the skills to attain better jobs and create a better future. Those with higher education as well as those who cannot afford higher education are making their mark in business-ownership—currently the largest number of people pursuing this goal. The higher education attainment and increased business-ownership are both altering the Latinos' economic status. Therefore, many Latinos have mainstreamed into the middle-class and even upper middle-class as a result.

This has affected the economy and will continue to do so, possibly pulling the U.S. out of this Great Recession of 2007-2010. Because of the newly found economic status, Latinos are gaining electoral ground, both in occupancy of political office and declaring their political voices in the 21st Century. And it will only improve from here. What the future holds for the Latino remains to be seen. Rapid change, continued population growth, and globalization shift the positioning of Latinos and place them in leadership roles that were once only a dream. Latino business leadership is rising; Latinos must prepare for the coming change.

Chapter 5
Viable Strategic Foresight Planning in Latino Business

E veryone knows that it is impossible to predict the future, at least with any accuracy. However, it is possible to make projections based on well-founded research. That is strategic foresight. Strategic foresight positions businesses to avoid any potential risk and be better prepared to take advantage of future opportunities. Strategic foresight is a crucial skill for decision makers to incorporate in their companies both old and new (Courtney, 2001). In strategic foresight planning, these things need to be rendered: a Trend Analysis, Scanning, Forecasting, Visioning, and Scenario Planning.

> *"In action be primitive; in foresight, a strategist.*
>
> *Ed Koch*

As stated above, it is impossible to make unequivocal predictions about the future. However, there are methods that can forecast a probable future. These include *trend impact analysis (TIA)* and *foresight planning.*

TIA is an uncomplicated approach to forecasting. It is a scanning method that provides a bird's eye view of future possibilities. This method of forecasting is a time series, modified to take into account perceptions regarding how future events may change extrapolations that would otherwise be surprise-free. When establishing a TIA, it is essential to specify the set of future events that could cause surprise-free trends to change in the future. A TIA is actually a database that lists a key of potential events, their probabilities, and their impacts (Gordon). It is a preparation method that helps anticipate a viable future for business.

Foresight planning will either start or involve scanning. Foresight planning is founded upon forecasts; forecasts are founded upon assumptions about the future. By scanning the horizon or the environment, one exercises prudence in identifying new developments that can challenge the past assumptions or provide new perspectives about the future threats or opportunities (Gordon & Glenn). Scanning is the skill of systematically searching the external environment to 1) best understand the nature and pace of change in the environment, 2) identify potential opportunities, challenges, and likely developments relevant to your organization.

Failure to anticipate can have disastrous consequences. Being astute by incorporating anticipatory management and gaining strategic advantage requires an element of sophisticated intelligence gathering techniques, new decision process models, and practical accountabilities. The gathering of such information will allow a company to capitalize on strategic outside intelligence. By incorporating anticipatory tools, companies avoid being blindsided by external forces, may profit from new opportunities, and may turn emerging threats into opportunities (Ashley & Morrison). We will discuss this at length and prove that to start or intend to improve a business without applying strategic foresight opens the organization for eventual failure.

Most of us would not imagine leaving home without a GPS when we are uncertain of how to reach a destination. Yet we navigate through business with blindfolds having no idea what's ahead, seeking to protect our businesses from danger or seize an opportunity that can alter the life of our business. Even ten years ago, the requirements for business success were not nearly as demanding as they are today. Strategic planning was as simple as developing a plan for where you wanted the company to go. Teams would assess the history of the company, see what was on hand, and a strategic plan was born. The 21st Century has transported us further than we could imagine into where predictive action must be taken. Even in these volatile and uncertain times we can look into the future, watch for trends, scan for threats and opportunities. From this, we can create possibilities and create the future we desire for our businesses. Today, technology has actually elevated the standards for how we plan our business, economy, and social future. We can actually anticipate and meet the future at the door and escort it in.

Strategic Planning

In the 1960s, corporate leaders embraced strategic planning as "the one best way" to devise and implement strategies that would enhance the competitiveness of business. According to the scientific management system pioneered by Frederick Taylor, it is the quintessential way to withdraw from performing and creating a new function staffed by specialists in strategic planning. These planning systems were expected to produce the best strategies in step-by-step instructions to follow those strategies so the implementers, the business managers, could have a clear blueprint that would help them accurately follow-up. Although in theory it was a flawless process, in practicality, it did not work out without deficits. The lesson was that strategic planning is not strategic thinking (Mintzberg, 1994). Strategic planning is developing a careful strategic direction and applying resources to pursue this strategy. To create a viable strategic plan, it is necessary to understand the current position and the possible avenues through which it can pursue a particular action. Generally strategic planning asks at least one of three questions (Pfohl, 2012):

- ➤ What do we do?
- ➤ For whom do we do it?
- ➤ How do we excel?

Thinking Strategically

Strategic thinking is the synergy of creativity, intuition, and the brainstorming of a Strategic Leadership Team (SLT). The thinking evolves into the vision which determines the direction an organization will go. Each of these team members comes into the SLT with unique cultural viewpoints and ideas which form strategic ideas. To those are added the culture of the organization—its set of beliefs, ideologies, and biases. Strategic leadership teams are established to collaborate in creativity and fulfilling organizational vision and change. Individuals incorporate their ideas from their perspective values and the viewpoints of their cultural beliefs. It is from one's belief system that one perceives the world and from which point one's thought process functions. By formulating a collective cohort with various and diverse viewpoints, a comprehensive strategic plan can be developed (Mintzberg, Ahlstrand & Lampel, 1998). In other words, gathering an SLT with similar viewpoints is fruitless to a good strategic plan. Empowered strategic leadership teams maintain the steady upward mobility essential to organizational growth. Despite the best strategic plans the 21st century has produced, there is now a need to look beyond the present and into the future to develop *strategic foresight plans.*

Introduction to Strategic Foresight

First, some definitions:

➢ *Foresight* is the knowledge or insight gained by or as by looking forward, a view of the future, prudence, foreseeing, foreknowledge, or prevision.

➢ *Forecasting* is the ability to predict (a future condition or occurrence); calculate in advance; plan beforehand.

➢ *Strategic Foresight* is a combination of forecasting with insight. It is developed by applying forecasting methods to insight and relating it to foresight of strategic issues. It can be developed by scien-tific study. It is not about intuition or guesswork.

"For tomorrow belongs to the people who prepare for it today."

African Proverb

The Art of Foresight

From strategic planning it was learned that for an effective plan an SLT was necessary for good strategic thinkers. Strategic thinkers who assist in developing strategic plans found that the plans were most effective (Mintzberg).

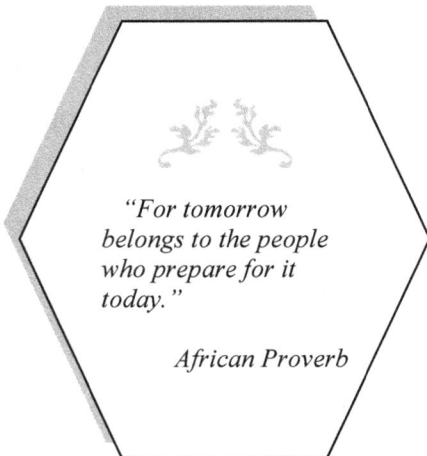

Today, there is another level to creating good strategic plans—Strategic Foresight Planning.

What is strategic foresight? Strategic foresight is a recent attempt to tease "futurology" from "futures studies." It emanates from the premise that: 1) the future is unpredictable 2) that it is not predetermined and 3) that future outcomes can be influenced by the choices we make in the present (Wikipedia). One thing is certain: without foresight we cannot prepare for the future. Foresight is and has been relevant to every part of human life. The difference is that today everything is changing at the speed of light. There is a notion that due to this age of hyperchange we are at a loss and have no idea what to prepare for. This uncertainty causes many people to think fatalistically and decide to do nothing!

In a World Future Society (WFS) report, it was stated that foresight offers increased power to shape our futures, even in the most turbulent of times. Thinking ahead offers the ability to have a much better life than your parents had, because you will be prepared to take advantage of all the new opportunities that our rapid social and technological progress has created. We are living in a different time; neglecting foresight by believing it is only in our mind is fatal to

> *"For tomorrow belongs to the people who prepare for it today."*
>
> *African Proverb*

business (WFS, 2004). When foresight is carefully applied, it offers protection from dangerous probabilities and provides

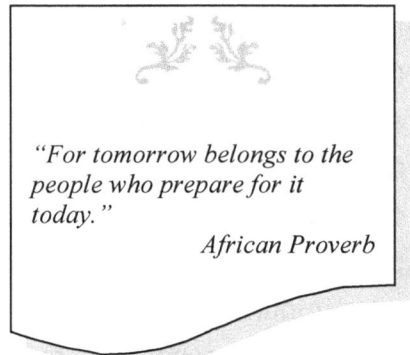

opportunities for future possibilities. People in business cannot afford *not* to apply strategic foresight to their business plans.

How can foresight be applied? It can be used to identify new products and services, as well as markets for those products and services. For foresight to be effective, the company has to be willing to make changes.

The more a company is willing to change, the more they should depend on foresight knowledge to provide the security for investment decisions (Jannek & Burmeister, 2007).

Small businesses can also use foresight in planning their strategies. If, for example, a local mom-and-pop grocery finds that the demographics in its neighborhood are changing, with foresight it will stock more foods linked to the neighborhood's ethnic tastes. An art museum director may want to follow trends in computer graphics to make exhibits more appealing to youth (WFS). A dentist with foresight may look into the latest equipment or new or improved techniques. A psychotherapist may want to use technology to expand her market. The benefit of foresight is that it may reveal potential threats you can prepare for before the situation becomes a crisis or exhibits opportunities that you may not have seen until it was too late. Foresight exposes the public's changing values and priorities, as well as emerging technologies, demographic shifts, economic con-straints or opportunities, and environ-mental and resource concerns. Each of these is a part of the increasing complex world system in which today's leader leads. It may sound frightful, but if you have foresight you will be vigilant about changing patterns.

Recognizing Patterns

Throughout this book, we have reiterated that the 21st Century has brought with it a whirlwind of rapid change. We have also discussed the various skills needed to operate in a world characterized by the rapidity of such changes. This segment will review how you can be perceptive, insightful, and highly productive in a world regulated by information. The topic of strategic

> *"Things can change so abruptly, so violently, so profoundly, that futures like our grandparents" have insufficient 'now' to stand on. We have no future because our present is too volatile. The spinning of the given moment's scenarios. Pattern recognition"*
>
> *William Gibson*

foresight planning is timely for the Latino business leader. It connects business development with vigilance and creates a panoramic view in an uncertain world. The merging of the two creates pattern recognition which we will refer to as trends analysis.

Whether you call it recognizing patterns, discovering trends, or what Hines & Bishop coined as "framing," the idea is to define the scope and focus of the issues requiring strategic foresight. The monitoring of trends is critical to every part of business; planning and marketing can be affected. Businesses are not isolated; they are a part of a larger ecosystem that is ever-changing.

As a leader, your role is to separate the background noise from what is vital. Here is where leaders must be careful to exercise wisdom. Trend analysis is used as the main methodology for better company models. Every industry and niche has experts dedicated to watch trends. Awareness of trends is not nearly as important as what can you do with the information relative to your company's strategic plan. Framing prevents misunderstandings that generate confusion and wasted work.

Most leaders can easily articulate the major trends of the day. Field and market research observations find that in most industries, leaders fail to recognize the less obvious yet profound ways that trends influence consumer's aspirations, attitudes, and behaviors (Ofek & Wathieu, 2010). Despite successes, it is critical to the life of your business to maintain a focus on what is ahead. The socioeconomic forces driving change today will evolve, requiring practical mechanisms to harness the available opportunities. Effective organizations understand the potential that partnership strategies offer not only to solve national challenges but also to create opportunities for socioeconomic growth and business success (Copulsky, et al., Business Trends 2013).

Environmental Scanning: The Hunt Begins

In ancient days, sailing ships had a "crow's nest" on the top of the mainmast. This enabled them to look out at sea to locate safe passage in uncharted waters. Today, it is believed we are moving towards uncharted waters ranging from global financial crisis and climate change to artificial biology and nano-technology. More than ever before we must identify change and assess its implications (Gordon & Glenn)—consequently, environmental scanning. Scanning is a mapping system which must be addressed as a global perspective, and businesses must take an intensive view of the issues (Hines & Bishop).

It is important to study the past so the wheel is not reinvented. When you look back, you assess both your successes and your failures. You look at your success as a stepping-stone into the future because you don't want to get stuck in the past (Hines & Bishop). Environmental scanning (ES), if you can imagine it, is like a hunt for clues about how the world is changing and how that change will affect your business. It is a discovery of leads, ideas, thought triggers, and data suggesting specific trends. Environmental scanning is a proven and powerful tool that leaders can use to study the circum-stances in which their company will be operating in the future. In

"Breadth + Depth = Foresight with Insight." Andy Hines

strategic foresight there are several steps that must be taken to develop a well-informed plan for the future of the business.

Environmental scanning begins that process. Once the decision makers understand that there are patterns or trends that are continually changing and that these changes merit monitoring, the process of *ES* can begin.

The key in ES is to scan the external environment for information useful to the company. Scanning is a relentless and ongoing process of looking for trends and events in the external environment that may have implications for the company. This search may lead to discovery of issues that the company can guard themselves against or it can be information that will prove itself useful (Hines & Bishop).

Environmental scanning is the careful monitoring of a business' internal and external environments (Strengths, Weaknesses, Opportunities, and Threats—the SWOT method); this detects internal strengths and weaknesses as well as the early signs of opportunities and threats that may influence its current and future plans. The surveillance is confined to a specific objective or a narrow sector (BusinessDictionary.com).

One method used is the Corporate Foresight (CF) system, which was created to establish foresight program studies that will support the achievement of a successful business. Another trend analysis method is the Trend Impact Analysis (TIA), an uncomplicated approach to forecasting.

Search for Opportunities and Eliminate Threats

This, of course, can be a daunting process if not for tools to simplify the task. The SWOT analysis is an excellent way to initiate strategy formation with a practical and uncomplicated tool that provides a comprehensive view of what your company faces. This technique simplifies your understanding of both the internal and external situations. With SWOT, you identify not only the internal operations of your company (strengths and weaknesses) but you also examine the external factors (opportunities and threats) that may have a direct effect on your company. When you use SWOT in your business it helps carve a sustainable niche in your market. There are so many opportunities available to companies that they cannot take. An evaluative process must then be demanded, for there are as many danger zones as there are opportunities.   There are several questions that you want to answer during your **SWOT** analysis:

- ➢ Internal Strengths:
  - ✓ What advantages does our company have?
  - ✓ What do we do better than anyone else?
  - ✓ What unique or lowest-cost resources can we draw upon that others cannot?
  - ✓ What do other people say our market strength is?

➢ Internal Weaknesses:
  ✓ What can we improve?
  ✓ What can we avoid?
  ✓ What do other people in our industry see as our weakness?
  ✓ What factors lose our sales?

➢ External Opportunities:
  ✓ What opportunities do you see?
  ✓ What trends are you spotting that you can take advantage of?
  ✓ What changes in social, technological, environmental, economic or political can we take advantage of?
  ✓ What changes in population, demography, or lifestyle can help expand our business?

➢ External Threats:
  ✓ What is the competition doing? (you must always know)
  ✓ What are the changes in quality, standards, and specifications in our products/services?
  ✓ Is technology threatening our position?
  ✓ Do we have debt or cash-flow problems?
  ✓ How badly can our weaknesses endanger our business? (MindTools.com)

Another similar method is the TOWS technique which takes an even closer look at what your business is up against. TOWS and SWOT are acronyms for different arrangements of the words Strengths, Weaknesses, Opportunities and Threats.

TOWS Strategic Alternatives Matrix

	External Opportunities (O) 1. 2. 3. 4.	External Threats (T) 1. 2. 3. 4.
Internal Strengths (S) 1. 2. 3. 4.	**SO** *"Maxi-Maxi" Strategy* Strategies that **use strengths** to **maximize opportunities.**	**ST** *"Maxi-Mini" Strategy* Strategies that **use strengths** to **minimize threats.**
Internal Weaknesses (W) 1. 2. 3. 4.	**WO** *"Mini-Maxi" Strategy* Strategies that **minimize weaknesses** by **taking advantage of opportunities.**	**WT** *"Mini-Mini" Strategy* Strategies that **minimize weaknesses** and **avoid threats.**

The TOWS matrix analyzes all the strategic choices you face to determine how you position yourself for success. It regulates how you: 1) make the most of your strengths; 2) circumvent your weaknesses; 3) capitalize on your opportunities; and 4) manage your threats. TOWS helps you match external opportunities and threats with your internal strengths and weaknesses, this way you have an even better description to organize your strategy.

Where SWOT and TOWS focus on analyzing your own business, the STEEP model, previously mentioned, offers a broader awareness of the industry (product/service) in which you operate.

Environmental scanning, like deep-sea fishing, is an in-depth search for information on trends that will enable businesses to build upon long-term innovative ideas for their present-day strategic plan. To efficiently use strategic foresight for businesses, you must ask three pertinent questions. These are broad questions, but each business will have a more specific answer and will narrow their answer as they the questions are explored (Van der Heijden):

➢ What is the key strategic issue for our company? (This is the framing question)

➢ What do we need to know about the issue? (These are the factors that will influence the decision)

➢ What are trends and drivers of change affecting these factors? (This is the focus for environmental scanning: industry specific, broad and global forces)

As specified in the previous chapter, there are certain force drivers of change that push for and then there are those that push against change.

Forecasting: Estimate the Climate Ahead

Most of us would not leave the house without listening to the weather forecast. The forecast determines what you will wear, how you will carry out your day, your mood, and how you perceive the way that day will go. Yet, a forecast is only an estimation based on historic patterns (trends) and information that has been well-researched that allow meteorologists to determine the weather for the day and the week. Even though the forecast is not always accurate, we prepare accordingly.

Futures forecasting is also a determination based on historic data that determine the direction of future trends. Forecasting is used to determine how to allocate budgets for near and distant future. Forecasts typically guide investors and banks to determine if events will affect a company, such as sales expectations. This can increase or decrease the price of company shares. It also helps provide an important benchmark for firms which have a long-term perspective of operations (Investopedia.com).

Forecasting allows companies to create alternate futures. What's unfortunate is that most companies believe that the future is going to mimic the past, and they often operate on a series of assumptions which tend to converge around incremental changes. Forecasting involves generating the widest range of creative possibilities, condensing and prioritizing the most appropriate for the company to actively consider or prepare as it moves forward. The best way to challenge the future is to develop alternative futures (Hines & Bishop).

The Driving Force Change: Uncertainty & Growth

Just as in Newton's third law of motion—"for every action there is an equal and opposite reaction," we can recreate Newton's 3rd law of "business." For every forecast that provides information on potential futures there is a disruptive dimension—calling into question assumptions about the present (Hines & Bishop). This calls analysts to recognize that effective foresight must be grounded upon an in-depth understanding of STEEP. The STEEP model gives a panoramic view at the problems that your industry, be it service or product, by taking five categories into account: Socio-cultural, Technological, Economic, Environmental, and Political aspects. This may bring to surface some of the problems that can affect the industry in which you operate. This menu of questions is not exhaustive and you may find that as you start asking the hard questions, it will open the door to even more topics of interest in each category. What you want to do here is focus on the key points to consider (Hines & Bishop).

Propagating Ideas

The best way to come up with great ideas often is to explore the obvious. Most solutions of today's problems are already available—just not yet discovered. The solutions are obvious. According to Hines & Bishop, most strategic issues and problems have been handled successfully in other fields and industries—so find out who they are. Examples: Hospitals discover new opportunities from car production; and banks learn strategic options from retailers; bio-strategists learn from nature; and science from fiction. Nature is the most successful organization in history—it has never experienced bankruptcy and it has performed efficiently. A science fiction writer's job is to create alternative futures and alternative realities (Hines & Bishop). With the ideas (strategic thinking) you can create several alternative futures.

Alternative Formation

Jane McGonigal is skilled in helping people reshape real life situations to the one situation they would prefer. She creates alternative realities through gaming. In her game, Chore Wars, she has reshaped the reality of chores into a competition. Chore Wars convinces you that you want to do the tasks. The game allows folks to choose their adventure and there is no mandatory chore, making you a voluntary participant in housework, strengthened because you must apply strategy to your housework adventure. She skillfully persuades gamers to create strategic planning, strategic thinking, and environmental scanning to come up with the alternative future of their choice

(McGonigal, 2011). Alternative conclusions are all possibilities. Data interpretation, while it can often give an accurate picture, is not always true. That requires more assumptions. Data can also have a bias interpretation to support the preconceived conclusion of the data collector (Hines & Bishop).

Strategic Visionary

Before we begin to create scenarios, we must convey the message in a way that's clear and concise. This is the only way that change agents can move forward. Peter Senge defines vision as "a picture of the future you seek to create, described in the present tense as if it were happening now." This vision must be conveyed so vividly the audience can smell it, touch it, and see it in the present (Hines & Bishop). Nancy Durante highlights both Steve Jobs and Martin Luther King, Jr. as the quint-essential speakers of our time. She recounts that the way they engaged their audience was through shifting from what is then immediately to what could be. MLK described the deficits in the way the nation had forfeited the rights of the Negro and then immediately transfers to what a world would look like if rights are restored. Then Jobs takes the audience through the journey of difficulties without Apple technology and rapidly moved to display what the world could be with Apple technology. Both these men were outstanding visionaries. Both managed to bring the audience through a journey and created a vivid visual of a future (Durante, TedX East).

Senge suggests that there are five potential starting points to creating vision. And these are (Hines & Bishop):

➢ Telling—decreeing the vision so everyone follows.

➢ Selling—knowing the vision, getting everyone to buy it.

➢ Testing—have an idea of the vision, wants to know population reaction prior to presenting.

➢ Consulting—gathering the vision and requesting input from audience.

➢ Co-creating—building the vision together through collaboration process.

When the vision is captured by the change agents then can the group proceed to creating the alternative futures which in this case is, scenario planning.

Creating Scenarios

Let the scenario planning begin. "Scenario planning is the practitioner's art" (Van der Heijden). By in large, you hear statements such as "life just happens" or "let the chips fall where they may" and "hey, we have no control over what happens in life." To some degree, this is true but this does not stop individuals from planning a wedding, a family the

"The future is not a place that we get to go... it is a place that you get to create."
Nancy Durante

purchase of a home, or saving for retirement. Not at all! They plan scenarios; they create a vision in the present of how the wedding will pan out, how many children they will have, where they will like to live, and where they want to retire. In its very basic form, all scenario planning is the same, except you will look at various scenes in your business for alternate futures.

By setting the framework through framing (recognizing patterns and trends) and scanning the environment, you've established the work context and knowledge base to support your goal. Then, forecasting lays out the panorama of potential futures to consider. Visioning depicts the preferred future and scenario planning creates the map to that preferred future (Hines & Bishop). Now, based on the previous findings, you can create that alternative future. Scenario planning will require developing a case for scenario-decision making—this will need an introduction to scenario-thinking and the actual scenarios can then be incorporated into the strategic management system (Ralston & Wilson, 2006).

Once the groundwork is prepared, you then begin to develop a set of alternative scenarios of comprehensive possible futures that describe each pragmatic scenario to decision makers. The scenarios must account for trends and driving forces, as well as uncertainties and their possible outcomes. Scenarios must be so comprehensive they can easily be applied in decision-making circumstances. Of course, the question then becomes how many scenarios can we create to efficiently find a desirable outcome? The range of possible futures is endless, but if too many scenarios are created, the effect will still leave one in chaos and confusion. Therefore, the experts learned that to accomplish the overall goal there should be no more than four scenarios (Ralston & Wilson).

To be efficient in presenting these futures it is best accomplished through story-telling. In this manner, each scenario renders a clear vision. The storylines need to be provocative and memorable, eliciting rich imagery. The exercise entails finding a way to develop the most interesting and enlightening stories. The scenarios need to be creative and pique interest; memorability will derive from originality. It is essential to remember that scenarios link to both historical and present events, yet they are hypothetical (van der Heijden).

Lastly, it is now time to act on the warnings of the scenarios. Scenarios, like any storytelling method, are embedded in "memories of the future" that enhance what businesses can recognize as relevant. They are rich arsenals of concepts. To take the scenario from decision to execution will require the participation of every member in the institution—and change is difficult. According to the theory of the learning cycle, scenario-based planning can lead to institutional learning only if it affects institutional action and feedback. Institutional action needs an enormous amount of consensus and/or compromise on what needs to be done. If the company succeeds in an organized process of a repetitive and cyclical learning loop, it will be more effective, adaptive, and/or an innovative player in its ever-changing environment (Galer and van der Heijden, 1992).

These are the formal steps in strategic foresight planning; however, for ultimate efficiency there needs to be a continuous cycle of learning. It is imperative that there be:

> No premature decision making.

> Permission for each participant to consider multiple perspectives/futures.

> A proactive attention for major uncertainties.

Likewise:

> Uncertainties should be stretched to the limit to explore implications

> Unusual alliances should be explored through development of consistent casual stories

> Unconnected ideas will be considered into a coherent framework

> Thinking time is permitted if ideas need to mature

Ideas and connections need to be repeatedly discussed and assessed informally. There needs to be a recycling of processes, systems, and methods. There need to be explicit and implicit processes and topics, key meetings, and decision points. Budgeting and project evaluations, strategy reviews, cost-cutting exercises, and product, capital, and market decision points also need be continuous (van der Heijden). This process can by no means be a one-time or sporadic event. Foresight planning needs to be a business style—which then leads us to anticipatory management.

Anticipation in Action

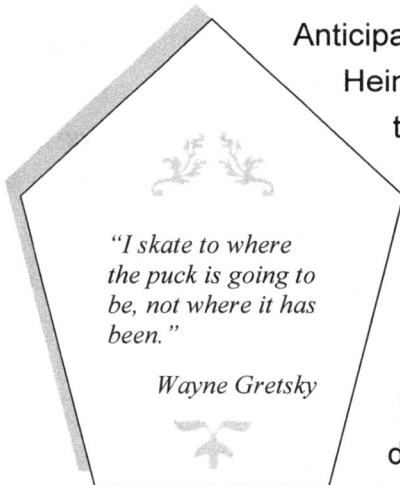

> *"I skate to where the puck is going to be, not where it has been."*
>
> *Wayne Gretsky*

Anticipation is not as we've known it in the Heinz commercial—waiting for something to happen. Today, anticipation has become proactive. Anticipatory Management allows the ability to leverage information across departments to facilitate a clear look into the future. It's much like business intelligence. Gone are the days of local market competition; introducing the new informational world. United States lived with the advantage of staying ahead of most countries—making America the land of opportunity; everyone came to find a piece of the pie. But the turbulent 70s and 80s knocked US business out with a huge blow, causing us to question our strategies, structures, culture, and purposes. The things that made us prosperous in the past and protected our domestic marketplace are no longer yielding success in this rapid, uncertain global marketplace. Now, US companies are competing globally against businesses that have inherent advantages over us, including natural and human resources, protective laws, and taxation policies. They have more modest lifestyles with more sophisticated philosophies and greater economic power. That leaves US businesses with the burden to out-think, out-anticipate our competitors if we have even a chance to out-perform them (Ashley & Morrison).

Paradigms are the lenses through which we observe the world. Paradigms define one's environment and anticipate behavior; they compose intelligence and one's understanding of the world. "The Paradigmatic Effect" is the contributing force in the failure of leaders to recognize change (Ashley & Morrison). Leaders often rely on their historical successes; therefore, they lack motivation to move towards change. This stifles personal and professional innovation. Change comes only through creativity, the movement to go beyond concepts. Innovation needs to be nurtured and applied (Molitor). In these turbulent times, failure to challenge implicit assumptions leads to strategic blindness. Paradigms are learned from organizational experiences, whether by formal training or from old habits, used in running the organization (Ashley & Morrison). Leaders who facilitate change, embrace new opportunities, and accept those opportunities are conditioned by a number of psychological factors, including the motivation to change, perceived need, communication patterns, attitudes, and forms of personal influence (Vago).

Management wants to anticipate what is going to happen next. There are two essential categories of information: 1) the environment that helps assess results and 2) game-changing (Hurwitz, 2011).

What do you want to assess in the environment? How successful was the last campaign? How many customers paid their bills on time? How much money is in the bank and how much do customers owe us? There is also the need to look across departments to understand not just what happened with customers in one product line but across product lines—and across

"Without a proper business response, the societal expectations of today become the political issues of tomorrow, legislated requirements of the next day and the litigated penalties the day after"

Ian Wilson

partners and suppliers. This is important, but it is also difficult. This kind of data requires having master data—a single definition of key components that define your company (Hurwitz, 2011).

Then there's game changing—here is where businesses would desire responses to these questions: What would customers want to buy next year? What would we do if we could anticipate our biggest weakness and fix it before it reaches crisis mode? This will be where information management will invest and innovate very soon.

Identify Emerging Issues

Ashley and Morrison have developed a model for conducting an emerging issue analysis. The title is self-explanatory but the model has several steps. The first step in the process is to identify emerging issues that can affect the company. As the magnitude of the signals increase, organizational options narrow and organizational liabilities increase. Consequently, the earlier emerging issues can be identified, the more options will be available. These tools can be used to identify emerging issues and where they are in their life cycle: scanning and monitoring processes, challenging assumptions, conducting issue vulnerability audits, and scenarios (Ralston and Wilson).

The Ramifications of Globalization to Latinos

As discovered previously, globalization is as ancient as the Bible. The forms of globalization have evolved over time but never at this accelerated rate. Distance is no longer an issue. The world is smaller and we can communicate globally in real time, travel in a fraction of the timeframe, and fall in love as well as do business globally with little or no obstacles.

Let us revisit the definition of globalization. Globalization describes an ongoing process by which regional economies, societies, and cultures have become integrated through a globe-spanning network of communication and trade. The global-ization term is often used to refer specifically to economic globalization: the integration of national economies into the international economy through trade, foreign direct investment, capital flows, migration, and the spread of technology.

Latinos are certainly equipped for the job in terms of their bilingual and bicultural status, where there is a deficit is in their lack of knowledge in strategic foresight planning. Once equipped with the tools and the training about how to structure their businesses for the future, they will understand that globalization has been seamed into the fabric of our future. Businesses that do not understand the ramifications of global competition and global interactions will fail miserably as a result.

The Connection: Strategic Foresight Planning &

Latino-Owned Business

As stated throughout these chapters the Latino population is growing and so is Latino-owned business. But Latino business ownership is a contemporary phenomenon. Individuals with foresight understand that the number of Latino entrepreneurs is rising and that in the next quarter century the numbers will be astronomical. In 1997, Astrid Chirinos had the foresight to begin a group for Latino professionals and entrepreneurs in Charlotte, NC, called "La Americas Business Council." Although at the time there were only 10,000 Latinos in the area, she understood that the population would explode shortly and she would be prepared for the influx. She prepared for the upcoming need with a larger infrastructure to deepen the available access, opportunities, and network possibilities. By 2001, the council name was changed to Latin American Chamber of Commerce (LACCC) having more than 400 members in an area that has populated to 100,000 Latinos and continues to grow (Hispanic Executive).

It is imperative that this brand new group of entrepreneurs prepare well for business with all the tools necessary for business success. By being equipped for the future with detailed scenarios for varying alternative futures and clear strategic foresight plans Latinos will be so well equipped in even the most uncertain future. Globalization will redirect the Latinos' stance and strategic foresight planning is how Latinos will understand where they go from here.

Chapter 6

The Spiritual Component of Latino Business

The United States was based on the inalienable right of governance through family, church and community, each rightfully sovereign within its sphere. This nation was founded on values of human dignity, legal equality, and personal freedom, all which reflect biblical values (Flax, Forbes). Without taking a political position, I think we can all agree that from the onset, we as a nation have grossly failed in upholding our bylaws. America has separated so vastly from what our forefathers built this nation upon that we are nearly unrecognizable. What revisionists deem as our greatest achievement—"Separation of Church and State"—is, in fact, our greatest downfall. Crosses are ripped down in parks, prayer is banished from schools, and the ACLU rampages to remove "under God" from the Pledge of Allegiance. "Separation of Church and State" is nowhere in the US constitution or any other legislation. Our forefathers were men of God who would have never sanctioned

"For I know the plans I have for you, plans to prosper you and not harm you plans to give you hope and a great future.

Jeremiah 29:11

the restrictions on religion extracted today (Flax). Yes, I believe in freedom of religion for all, but that is not what is currently happening in our nation today.

You will find that throughout this chapter there will be many scriptural quotes. These scripture are used to reveal that scripture has a model for business success. Throughout the bible possibly has the most information on how to succeed in business covering every detail thoroughly.

We now find ourselves with lives that are compartmentalized, with each compartment in a neat little box and no box touches the next. We have our family life, our work life, our spiritual life; and on occasion we have a secret life and we go to great lengths to keep them separate. The truth is that if there is any imbalance in any 'compartment,' it will inevitably affect all others. The idea that we can separate our spiritual selves from our professional selves is a fallacy. We were created as whole beings and any attempt to separate any part of our being cannot work and will become a stressor.

Patricia Aburdene submits that spirituality in the workplace is a powerful trend transforming capitalism. Her viewpoint is that divine presence spills into business and it can actually transform companies. This information has resulted in many Fortune 500 companies incorporating spirituality into their work environment (Aburdene, 2005). If compartmentalization continues to be the school of thought, then why the sudden change in belief that spirituality even belongs in business? There is an extensive list of important perspectives. Some believe that spirituality is simply the embodiment of values, honest, integrity, and good quality work. For others, it is about treating coworkers and employees in a caring manner. Still for others, it's participation in spiritual study groups, using prayer, meditation, or intuitive guidance at work. Then there are those who are making their business socially responsible for how it impacts the environment, serves the community, or helps create a better world (McLaughlin, Sri Aurobindo Society).

In this chapter, we will explore how cultivating God-centered spirituality at the work-place can actually trans-form businesses. There will be several references to great leaders with spiritual, leadership, and business platforms. There will also be references to the biblical perspectives on how to run, grow, and succeed in business. You will be surprised at how much God's word has to say about today's organization. You will also be amazed at how this ancient book goes into depth about marketing ethics, stewardship, ethics, and how to be an effective servant leader when transforming your organization with biblical viewpoints (Winston, 2010). This will position you miles ahead in your business and industry.

"Do not conform to the pattern of this world, but be transformed by the renewing of your mind.

Romans 12:2

Spirituality in the workplace is the one ingredient that changes every aspect of business. We will review each of the prior chapter subjects and make the connection as to the impact spirituality can have in each of these areas. We will also look at the impact on Latino business in areas of leadership styles, EQi, core values and ethics, drivers of change, and how to have a clear picture for foresight strategy planning. The spiritual aspects of each will be merged.

Spirituality in the Workplace: A New Trend or Real Discovery?

What does "spirituality in the workplace" even mean? According to McLaughlin, "spirituality in business" means different things to different people. How do you know when you have it right? How do you know if you have clearly reached your quest for spirituality in business? Marques and Dhiman tell a poignant story which goes like this: *"One day a man came across three stonecutters working in a quarry. Each was cutting out a block of stone. Curious, he asked the first stonecutter what he was doing. 'What? Are you blind?' the stonecutter shouted 'Can't you see, I am cutting this stupid stone.' Shocked but none the wiser, the man turned to the second stonecutter and asked*

"As the deer panteth after the water, so my soul panteth after thee, O God."

Psalms 42:1

him what he was doing. 'I am cutting this block of stone to make sure that its sides are straight and smooth so the builder can build a straight wall.' Feeling a lot better but still really not any wiser, the man turned to the third stonecutter, who seemed the happiest of the three, and asked him what he was doing. 'I am building a cathedral,' the third stonecutter replied." Although "spirituality in business" is increasingly being embraced it is most important to know what spirituality in business is and how you know you have achieved your attempt.

In an era of unbelief, most old theological words remain long after the faith that gave them meaning is gone. Carl Jung, the great psychotherapist of the 1930s went on a quest to find the cure for alcoholism through psychotherapy. After all his best efforts, he wrote a letter to Bill W. and concluded that "The evil principle prevailing in this world leads the unrecognized spiritual need into perdition. It's not counteracted either by real religious insight or by the protective wall of human community." In his letter, he continued stated that an ordinary man who is not protected by an action from above and isolated from society cannot resist the power of evil. But to use such words, he stated, arouses so many mistakes that one can only stay as aloof as possible. Alcoholism in Latin is "spiritus," the same word used for the highest religious experience as well as for the most depraving poison. This formula, Jung attests, is "spiritus contra spiritum" (Jung, 1930). The need for connection with the creator has not changed. Even if for many alcoholism may not be the "spiritus" of choice, workaholism is a parallel poison. The array of "isms" is endless, all caused by the craving for spiritual connection.

The pressure of work, family, the economy, and the effort to maintain a healthy spiritual life has become overbearing for most. According to WebMD, high levels of stress or being under long-term stress can cause continual sickness and eventually lead to long-term health problems such as heart disease, high blood pressure, back problems and depression. It can also cause headaches, trouble sleeping, problems concentrating, short temper, upset stomach, job dissatisfaction, and low morale (WebMD). In contrast, spirituality has many benefits for stress relief and overall mental health. It helps by giving a sense of purpose, connection to the world, release control, expansion of a support network, and a healthier life. This may be why so many Fortune 500 companies have chosen to allow spirituality in the workplace to be incorporated into the fabric of the company (Aburdene, 2005). McLaughlin asserts that there is an increase in business leaders who've concluded that there is more to life—and business—than profits alone. Money as the sole bottom line (final result) is becoming a thing of the past. The new trend says it's all about bringing your spiritual values into your workplace (McLaughlin, 2009).

The Emerging Paradigm (Pattern)

Spirituality in the workplace is an emerging pattern that is expressed in many ways. Some say that there is a fundamental tension between rational goals and spiritual fulfillment. Some say that people want to find meaning in their work, and others hold that something has been stirring in workers' souls for connection, greater simplicity, and a connection with something higher. Marques and Dhiman cite Bruce Jentner from Jentner Financial Group as stating that "I have a deep conviction that everybody needs something bigger in life than just making money and going to work" (Marques & Dhiman).

Organizational scientists can no longer avoid analyzing, understanding, and treating organizations as spiritual entities. Organizations must become more spiritual if they are to serve the ethical needs of their stakeholders. In an in depth study done by Mitroff and Denton, it was estimated that organizations that identified more strongly with spirituality or had a greater sense of spirituality had employees who 1) were less fearful of their organizations, 2) were less likely to compromise their basic beliefs and values in the workplace, 3) perceived their organizations as significantly more profitable, and 4) reported that they could bring significantly more of their complete selves to work, specifically their creativity and intelligence—two qualities that essential to the success in today's hypercompetitive environment. In their comparison of those organizations that considered themselves more spiritual and those who considered themselves less spiritual—the more spiritual scored higher (Mitroff and Denton, 1999). There is something to be said for those companies which allow spirituality to be at the center.

Hughes posits that intellectual creativity, such as thinking new thoughts, developing new insights, and creating new and fresh ways of understanding old material is in direct connection to the pursuit of truth. The biblical perspective offers little tolerance for "the life of the mind" or a competing worldview and perspectives (Hughes). There is evidence of a lack of leadership and resources provided by the church about the integration of faith and the workplace. There seems a correlation between work satisfaction and the integration of faith. Walker cites Miller as attesting to what he coined the "Four E Integration Types: in the order of EX = Experiential, EV = Evangelization, EN = Enrichment, and ET = Ethical" (Walker, 2005). Roman Catholics have been very successful in integrating faith into their very rich intellectual heritage. They have mastered the integration of faith and the sustenance of the mind (Hughes p. 43-45). If a person's faith is not from a religious experience but the core of who that person is, then despite the environment, the truth of Christ will reverberate.

"Remember the Lord your God, for it is he who gives you the ability to produce wealth, and so confirms his covenant which he swore your ancestors, as it is today"

Deuteronomy 8:18

Spirituality in Business Boosts Revenue Streams

With spirituality comes a change in the quality of individuals you attract and retain. So the question then becomes this: are spirituality and profitability incompatible? According to a body of researchers, what you do by opening the company to ethics and spiritual values is you will be led to increased productivity and profitability as well as employee retention, customer loyalty, and brand reputation. Spirituality also encourages a boost to your company and it enhances morale (Dr. Pratik P. Surana).

People that have had great success in merging faith and business and running their organizations audaciously through scripture and biblical principles include John Maxwell, Os Hillman, Simon Bailey, and Dani Johnson. The Catholic Church has also proven success in this integration. Hughes questions what it would mean to teach from a Christian perspective and the apprehension of not exploiting the educational system by transforming lectures into pulpits. One may agree that attempting to Christianize staff, vendors, or followers is not the wisest way to run an organization (Hughes). But by using biblical perspectives, you, the leader, can guard your character—the essence of a great leader. It should be that the separation of one's faith from one's business is impossible since core values and integrity are intertwined with faith. Christian leaders may not be speaking on pulpits with podiums but their values and actions are on display and are carefully examined by others. Therefore, as Christian leaders, the life of the mind needs always to demonstrate *agapáo* love.

Yet another Leadership Shift: The Spiritual Twist

This chapter navigated through the Latinos in America past, present, and where it's projected they will be in the future. It concluded that the one thing that distinguishes Latinos is their innate ability to work hard, be dependable, loyal, and have high integrity. As said previously in the book, although it is impossible that every single member of a group ascribes to every attribute or virtue, we speak of the cultural group as a whole. There are also the bicultural, bilingual attributes and the fact that Latinos are a collective society.

Many Latino characteristics have aspects of servant leaders due to their strong spiritual beliefs. Although many leaders have an innate ability to lead, quintessential leadership must be developed. Throughout this book, we have stated that we are experiencing rapid change like never before.

"Good leaders must first become good servants.

Robert Greenleaf

The earth is chattering beneath us and uncertainty is the only thing that is now certain. This change and this uncertainty may be responsible for the change in followers. People no longer want to be led by autocratic leaders; they desire to have a voice and be respected for their contribution. They wish to exercise their rights. This calls for a different kind of leader.

Power and authority are now being reexamined and people are beginning to learn to relate to one another in a less coercive, more creative, and supporting manner. There is a new emergence of moral principle which holds that the only authority worthy of one's devotion and fidelity is that which is freely and knowingly granted by the led to the leader. The issue is that those who follow this principle will no longer accept the authority of the existing institutions. As a result, followers who support this principle will follow only those leaders who are proven and trusted as servants. This principle will be common in the future and the only companies that will be viable will be those that are predominantly servant led (Greenleaf, 1977).

Victor Hugo once said, "There is nothing as powerful as an idea whose time has come." Servant leadership's time has now come! What is a servant leader? In Greenleaf's foreword, Stephen Convey asserts that at the depth of human nature is that which urges people—each of us—to rise above our present circumstances, to transcend our common nature. And if a leader can appeal to it, you've tapped into a new source of human motivation. (Greenleaf, 1977).

What is a Servant Leader?

The servant leader philosophy can be disturbing until you truly understand what a servant leader is. We have been taught as children not to follow but to lead, yet no one taught us how to be successful leaders. Servanthood has always been interpreted as the lowliest of jobs; be a servant and a leader seems like an oxymoron to most.

The servant leader philosophy proposes that the leader is a servant first. It is a desire and conscious choice to serve, which later manifests one to aspire to lead. This concept is in direct contrast to the leader who desires to lead first—the passion to lead may then be a self-centered desire, whereas if a servant first, the leader has the experience of servant and can therefore lead better. The leader first and the servant first are polar opposites—with shadings and blends that are part of the infinite variety of human nature. The difference is embodied in the care taken by the servant-first who ensures that other people's highest priority needs are met. An example of good servant leadership is when there is evidence of growth in the followership (or employees) and the followers become healthier, wiser, freer, more autonomous, and more likely to become servant leaders themselves. Greenleaf submits that servant leadership can be manifested by individuals as well as businesses and other organizations as a whole (Greenleaf, 1998). To be a servant leader you must humbly submit to (acknowledge, and appreciate) employees in a way that they feel secure that the leader is aligned with them and supportive. When employees feel safe they respond with loyalty and respect for their leadership. As with any cause and effect what a servant leader propels is employee satisfaction, therefore, greater productivity. A servant leader understands that good customer service begins with good employee service. As the great Zig Ziglar said "You can have everything in life that you want if you just give enough other people what they want."

Leadership—the Biblical Perspective

Although not typically called the guideline for outstanding leadership, the Bible clearly delineates great leadership. In the Book of Acts, Paul reminds leaders that they have a responsibility to be mindful of their motives and to take care of people that they oversee. Paul was very precise in his details of what qualified a great leader. He was also clear that if leaders did not have the specific qualities, they were to be excluded from leadership roles (Titus 1:5-9). Leadership is a responsibility and not a title. Having a following—either as a business leader or a politician—makes you the leader liable for the safety of your employees/followers. People rely on leaders to be their spokesperson and act with their best interests at heart.

"Be on guard for yourselves and for all flock, among which you have been made an overseer."

O'Toole brilliantly made the link in what he coined the "Rushmorean model." He fashioned this model from the four leaders in Mount Rushmore. He described these four representatives in the school of values-based leadership, dedicated to democratic change. Although these four leaders were not flawless leaders, they shared similar leadership value characteristics as Jesus, virtues such as: courage, authenticity, integrity, vision, passion, conviction, and persistence. All four portrayed inspired trust and hope in their followers and led change, qualities critical to the personification of a Jesus-like leadership style. Rushmorean leaders impart values such as integrity, trust, listening, and respect for followers into their organizations. They developed change through the pursuit of moral ends that their followers could adopt as their own; these ends derived from the real needs of their followers (O'Toole). Leaders have a moral and ethical obligation to lead with love. They must exercise what Winston depicts as *agapáo* love; to do the right thing at the right time for the right reason in a social or moral sense, embracing the judgment and the deliberate assent of the will as a matter of principle, duty, and propriety (Winston 2002).

Synergizing Spirituality and Business

It can be argued that in a leadership role it is important to walk with caution, conscious that there are guidelines for such responsibility. Again we cannot compartmentalize the marketplace and separate spirituality from our leadership responsibility. Therefore, as spiritual leaders we are obliged to employees, customers and vendors; and the marketplace is our ministry. We desperately need Christian businesses that go beyond simply pursuing honesty by, paying taxes, and keeping Playboy magazine out of the men's room. If we were paying attention, our economists would have blown John Maynard

Keynes and his debt-driven money system fiat out of the water (Peacocke, 2002). Leaders have a responsibility to synergize spirituality in the workplace; it all begins with the leader. Spirituality in the workplace cannot even begin without a leadership that manifests servant leadership, because, as the leader goes, so goes the organization" (Malphurs, 1998).

Funneling Emotional Intelligence and Spirituality

"But the fruit of the Spirit is love, joy, peace, patience, kindness, goodness, faithfulness, gentleness, self-control; against such things there is no law." Galatians 5: 22-23

When discussing Emotional Intelligence (EI), we drew these conclusions: 1) two leadership styles have proven higher EQi scores and 2) Latinos score higher in EQi than in IQ. Mills asserts that the transformational leadership concept may provide a model for the relevance of emotions to leadership. Bass and Avolio's report there are four dimensions of transformational leadership: idealized influence, inspirational motivation, intellectual stimulation and individualized consideration—these leadership skills are intertwined with the concepts of emotional intelligence. Mills suggests that EI may now be considered a component of leadership effectiveness. This leadership style supports greater levels of leadership effectiveness (Mills, 2009).

The other leadership style that proves high EQi scores is Servant Leadership. Theorists propose that an outstanding leader is a servant leader—servant leaders have proven to have the best outcomes with employees/followers. Hannay and Fretwell report that the servant leadership theory goes beyond traditional trait, behavioral, and situational theories.

The servant leadership style is unique and selfless and requires an individual willing to place the focus on promoting others (Hannay & Fretwell).

A Leader with High EQi is Confident

To be an effective leader, you—the leader—must know who "you are." Jesus knew who He was and what his assignment was. Therefore, all he had to do was ensure it was accomplished. Jesus had a visual of his efforts when He said "I declare a thing and it is done for me. My Word accomplishes what I sent it out to do" (Isaiah 55:11). He said things like, "I always do what pleases God" (John 7:29) and "God always answers my prayers" (John 11:42). It might seem that Jesus suffered from conceit, yet He is described as one of the most humble beings whoever walked the earth. Further, He was also one of the most confident men who ever lived. Belief in oneself is a crucial quality of leadership. A leader who vacillates sends an uncertain message; people grow uneasy and lose confidence (Jones, 1992).

A Leader with High EQi Inspires Growth

According to the Emotional Intelligence philosophy, leaders with high EQi scores have the characteristics that inspire followers to commit to a shared vision and goals. They do this by challenging people to become innovative problem solvers and do things greater than themselves, while providing support. One of Jesus' innate abilities was to ask people to follow him, and they would drop what they were doing and follow him. Witness Peter and the Samaritan woman. Historically, you will find that people hunger for something larger than themselves; and leaders who offer that have no shortage of followers (Jones). In fact, a higher purpose is such a vital element of the human psyche that scripture asserts that "where there is no vision, the people perish" (Proverbs 29:18). If your vision for your followers/employees is greater than what they can see, they will achieve it because *you* believe they can.

A Leader with High EQi Loves His Followers

Love has been so misunderstood and contorted that it has been reduced to a sexual act. Yet, love is the infrastructure for everything and anything of value. For three years, all Jesus spoke about was "love."

> *"And above all these put on love, which binds everything together in perfect harmony.*
>
> *Colossians 3:14*

There is a legend that goes like this: "John, the disciple whom Jesus loved, being quizzed repeatedly by the crowd of eager young converts about heavenly principles, tells the crowd, 'Little children, love one another.'

'That's great, John, but how do we heal the sick as Jesus did?' asked an eager young man.

John repeated, 'Little children, love one another.'

'Okay, John, we get the point but how can we become truly great leaders?' asked the crowd.

John rose again and said quietly, 'Little children love one another'" (Jones).

It may seem over-simplified but if a leader does not exercise "agapáo" love in a social and moral sense, embracing the judgment and the deliberate assent of the will as a matter of principle, duty, and

"A good name is to be chosen rather than great riches, and favor is better than silver or gold.

Proverbs 22:1

propriety, then he does not *have* "agapáo." What "agapáo" means to today's leaders is the consideration of the hu-man and

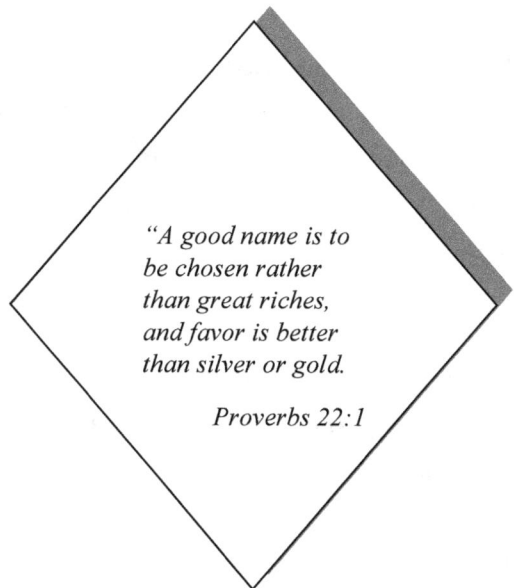

spiritual aspects of their employees / followers (Winston). This is the ultimate EQi score.

Core Beliefs and Values Founded on Spiritual Principles

Eerie is the day when you suddenly learn that a person or institution which you believed upheld the highest integrity has deceived you, your family, your community, or/and the world. We reached that day in October, 2001, when the Enron Corporation, an American energy company based in Houston, Texas, bankrupted and the auditing firm Arthur Anderson was found in collusion. Enron's stock went from nearly $91 per share to $1 per share in less than thirty days.

In a post-Enron world, values and ethics are urgent concerns. What has become all the rage today is the "triple bottom line," a commitment to "people, planet, and profit." The paradigm shift is now focused on employees and the environment is perceived as important as economics. The buzz is that it's all about bringing your spiritual values into your workplace (Corrine McLaughlin).

You'll Find It in The Character

A. W. Tozer defines character as strength of moral fiber. He describes character as the "excellence of moral being." High standards in values and ethics define a person's character, which is exhibited in honesty, ethics, and benevolence. Assertions of character are principles and integrity. A person of flawed character exhibits moral deficiency, dishonesty, and unethical behavior.

Then in March of 2002, Adelphia Communications, the country's largest cable company, reported that it too had financial problems. The founder, John Rigas, with his three sons, were accused of using company assets as collateral for loans totaling $3.1 billion to make personal purchases and finance family projects. On that very day, Dennis Kozlowski, CEO of Tyco, was charged with evading $1 million in sales taxes on artwork and other items he had bought for himself with company funds. In a poll conducted by Time/CNN—most Americans fear that they see not merely a few isolated cases, but a pattern of deception by a many companies. And that was before the WorldCom internal audit that found improper accounting procedures.

All this has spawned distrust. Zig Ziglar stated in a letter he wrote to John Maxwell: ". . .according to the Thomas Jefferson Research Institute, in the days when the founding fathers were growing up, over 90 percent of the educational thrust was of a moral ethical, religious nature. By the 1950s the percentage of that same educational thrust was so small it could not be measured" (Maxwell, 2003).

Organizational Values

Values are vital to any organization's culture—the very threads that comprise the organizational fabric. The single most important feature of any corporation is its system. Any company that overlooks the importance of core values does so to its detriment. Values are a critical component of business in many ways. There are essential reasons why core values are so important to business. Values determine company distinctives, dictate personal involvement, communicate positive change, influence overall behavior, inspire people to action, enhance critical leadership, shape corporate character, contribute to business success, and affect strategic planning. Values drive the organization. Values affect decision making, direction and goal setting, conflict resolution, company satisfaction, company commitment, problem solving and priorities determination. Values deeply affect roles of clarification, team building, monitoring, evaluation, rewards and recognition of workers; financial management and resource utilization. There is virtually no area exempt from the impact of company values (Malphurs, 2004).

The Biblical Viewpoint

The Bible makes many references to spiritual character. In Proverbs 6: 16-19, it tells what things God hates: *". . .haughty eyes, a lying tongue, hands that shed innocent blood, a heart that devises wicked plans, feet that make haste to run to evil, a false witness, and one who sows discord among followers."* A person's character is predicated upon their general tendencies and isolated actions.

You will know people's values through their characters. Their characters are the sum of their thoughts, intentions, disposition, desires, and actions. *"Keep your conduct among the Gentiles honorable"*—I Peter 2:12; *"Let your reasonableness be known to everyone"*—Philippians 4:15, and *"For where your treasure is, there your heart will be also"*—Matthew 6:21. Then you will have *". . .sound wisdom; I have insight; I have strength"*—Proverbs 8:14.

Drivers of Change—the Spiritual Factor

To death and taxes we must add another certainty of life—change. Nothing ever stays the same and it's been that way since the beginning of time. In chapter IV we determined that the drivers of change have repositioned the Latino population to achieve the long-desired American dream. The shift has been slowly placing Latinos in the mainstream of the middle class. The Information Age brought the world closer and caused the melding of international interaction in real time from your desk. Companies are fusing relationships, expanding internationally, and competing globally for

> *"For everything there is a season, and a time for every matter under heaven."*
>
> *Ecclesiastes 3:1*

the same audience. And all this is caused by the drivers of change. But there is a spiritual factor that propels these changes and repositions people for success.

Biblical Accounts of Change

If you believe that everything has a spiritual element—as I do—then change is also manipulated by the spirit. We will begin with the biblical accounts of change. Each time you find a repositioning of a population it follows a time of mistreatment of a population.

Egyptian empire—in Genesis 37, the Bible begins with an account of Joseph, a Jew, and his journey to become second-in-command to Pharaoh in Egypt. We learn that Joseph interpreted the Pharaoh's first dream, which resulted in Pharaoh's being the only one prepared for famine. The existence of food allowed Pharaoh to rule the entire Middle East. It also resulted in Joseph's family settling in Egypt as did many Jews during this famine. Exodus 1: 1-22 chronicles that the number of Jews grew massively. But then Egypt experienced a change in pharaohs. While scripture doesn't name either pharaoh, the first may have been Ramses, and scholars believe the second—the one that was in office during the exodus, was Tutmose II.

The new pharaoh, to whom Joseph meant nothing, became anxious of the growing number of Jews; he feared that if there was war they could overthrow his kingdom—so he made them slaves. They were slaves for four hundred years. In Exodus 2—Moses is born with a purpose—God's purpose—to free the Jews from captivity. He is born in Egypt and is cared for by Pharaoh's daughter. He would later leave Egypt for forty years. In Exodus 5, Moses returned to Egypt to seek release of the Jews from captivity; but things became worse for the Jews before they got better. After a long series of plagues, in Exodus 12, Pharaoh allows the exodus of the Israelites. Exodus tells that the Israelites left with all the wealth of Egypt—payment and interest accrued for the 400 years of slavery. This was the first repositioning of a population. The Egyptian empire fell and the Israelites relocated to a land rich with milk and honey–after navigating in the desert for forty years.

Babylonian empire—2 King 25:1—6 reports that in 597 BC, Nebuchadnezzar, King of Babylon, invaded Judah by seizing Jerusalem, breaking through the walls and conquering the city. Zedekiah, King of Judah, was captured. His sons were killed in front of him, then he was blinded and taken captive to Babylon. Jerusalem was plundered. Solomon's Temple and all the homes in Jerusalem were destroyed. Most elite in the country were taken captive. The poorest people were left behind to work the vineyards and the fields. Guards were left to monitor their work.

Nebuchadnezzar's armies took all the valuables of the temple: the bronze, pots, shovels, wick trimmers, and dishes made of gold and silver. The Israelites were in exile in Babylon for seventy years. The Babylonian empire fell and the Persian King Cyrus freed the Israelites to go back to Israel and restore Solomon's temple. Ezra 2 tells that 772,174 Jewish men were freed, plus their wives, children, livestock and goods, a further repositioning of a population.

Recent Accounts of Change

German empire—Adolf Hitler was appointed Chancellor of Germany in 1933. The Weimar Republic was concerned about how it would come out of the depression; the Nazis promised to solve the problem. Initially, Hitler was not taken seriously by most people. They were certain he could not possibly last. But as one action after the other was met with an amazing measure of success, amusement was transformed into incredulity. The world thought it inconceivable that such things could happen in this modern civilization. And Hitler, the leader of these activities, was viewed as an inhumane madman (Toland, 1976). He used the Jews and other sections of society as scapegoats, and he blamed all the nation's problems on them. Germans were so desperate for answers that Hitler's insane solutions started to make sense. He was also very shrewd in that he created camaraderie among people. He found people's fear and seized the opportunity.

Hitler manipulated his high-rank to gain absolute power over Germany. Then on August 2, 1934, Paul von Hindenburg (the Kaiser) died; Hitler then took the title of Fuhrer and Reichskanzler (Leader and Reich Chancellor). He increased

Germany's military power and in March of 1938, he annexed Austria to Germany. Nazi Germany attacked Poland in September, 1939, and the surrounding European nations declared World War II. Germany was losing the war and despite Hitler's preparing the Nazis to fight to the death, many defected. On April 29, 1945, Hitler married his longtime mistress and on April 30, they both committed suicide. The global war was over in 1945. The Jews started being released from the concentration camps in January, 1945 but many were still being released until May 1945 (Giblin, 2002). This was another driver of change that repositioned a population from oppression to and over a short period of time to success.

African-Americans—in the 1960s, America still struggled with inequality. Martin Luther King, Jr. saw a need that became his desperate passion. He desired what the scripture and his country had promised, "liberty and justice for all," and he knew this kind of liberty was not equally distributed.

America was not ready for the social change that was about to take place. It was probably the most difficult civil war for the Caucasian American to fight—this was its first experience of resistance without hatred. There was a war without anger—and a rightful indignation without fists, weapons and at times without even words.

MLK taught people to get what belongs to them without the anger, bitterness, or hatred and did this through scripture. He took scripture and taught that you can win a war without blood.

The scripture was the source and the spiritual intervention that propelled social change. His vision for change was equality for all. As a man of faith, he protested and rallied, but all in peace. He took the biblical principles and what the Bible spoke about freedom, racism, discrimination, and prejudice and fought for the rights that he had as a citizen and what he believed as a child of God. MLK challenged Americans on scriptural principles:

Psalms 82:3-4—*Give justice to the weak and the orphan; maintain the right of the afflicted and the destitute. Rescue the weak and the needy; deliver them from the hand of the wicked.*

Proverbs 21:3—*Do what is right and just; that is more pleasing to God than sacrifice.*

Isaiah 1:16-17—*Wash yourselves; make yourselves clean; remove the evil of your doings from before my eyes; cease to do evil, learn to do good; seek justice, correct oppression; defend the fatherless, plead for the widow.*

Matthew 5:3-12—*Blessed are the poor in spirit for theirs is the realm of heaven. Blessed are those who mourn for they shall be comforted. Blessed are the meek for they shall inherit the earth. Blessed are those who hunger and thirst for righteousness, for they shall be filled.*

Colossians 3:12-14—*Put on then, as God's chosen ones, holy and beloved, compassion, kindness, lowliness, meekness, and patience, forbearing one another and, if one has a complaint against another, forgiving one another; as God has forgiven you, so you also must forgive. Above all these put on love, which binds everything together in perfect harmony.*

2 Peter 3:13—*What we await are new heavens and a new earth where, according to God's promise, the justice of God will reside.*

Martin Luther King, Jr., was a man of power, yet a gentle man of conviction, a nonviolent man who stood on principles—God's principles. He had a strong conviction, but it was his faith that infused his ability to stand and make a difference. It was a long, hard fight that eventually took his life—but he got the desired outcome—liberty and justice for all. He made many speeches that to-date resonate with most Americans. And he made several quotes that speak clearly why violence is not a resolve.

"You may murder the liar, but you cannot murder the lie, nor establish the truth. You may murder the hater, but you do not murder hate, nor establish love. Returning violence for violence multiplies violence, adding deeper darkness to a night already devoid of stars." —Martin Luther King, Jr.

"Darkness cannot drive out darkness, only light can do that. Hate cannot drive out hate; only love can do that." —Martin Luther King, Jr.

Drivers of Change the Spiritual Factor—change is always driven by spiritual factors and once we understand this we are more aware and can make wiser choices. Standing up for what is correct based on biblical principles is yields the best outcome.

Latinos are Now Driving Change

It is clear—the jury is in. The repositioning of the Latino population is on its way to achieving the long-desired American dream. It is now it is now their turn to lead. Latinos have had a long road of low socioeconomic struggles, while assimilating and acculturating the way Americans expected. This has, for many years, been the contention and the reason Latin Americans have not been accepted as Americans. Yet the time has come—the Latinos refusal to discard their culture has now resulted in their being the most equipped for globalization. International communication needs individuals who are linguistically and culturally equipped. Latin American countries are also coming up in rank and they are ready to do business internationally. Hence, the perfect strategic alliance!

Adding a spiritual component to this cultural sensitivity makes the Latino the most logical choice for leadership. Latinos have, unknown to anyone and often even themselves, been in preparation for this change. And since spirituality has been so ingrained in the culture, it makes this integral characteristic natural to incorporate into their businesses. Latinos have had a God-centered belief that has seeped into their culture, values, ethics and the drivers of change are also changing their economic status.

Spirituality in Foresight Planning

In Chapter 5, we determined that the Latino population is rapidly growing and so are Latino-owned businesses. Latino business ownership is a contemporary phenomenon and not typical for Latinos due to their low socioeconomic position. This shift in Latino entrepreneurs is rising and in the next quarter century the numbers of Latino business will be leading astronomically. It was concluded that Latinos must use foresight strategies not only to create businesses but also to position themselves as leaders in the community, organizationally, and in government. Latinos should equip for the future with detailed scenarios for varying alternative futures, and clear strategic foresight plans. Latinos will be well equipped in even the most uncertain future. Then we finalized the segment with how globalization will redirect the Latinos' stance and strategic foresight planning to help Latinos decide where they can go from here.

Explore American history and you will find that in several instances where Americans failed to anticipate the future. This is a continual cause for concern. Pearl Harbor was a clear indication of lack of anticipatory intelligence. In extracts from an American report on the attack on Pearl Harbor in 1941, it chronicles, "the underlying cause of this error of judgment was General Short's confidence that Japan would not attach Pearl Harbor" (LearningCurve.Gov). Again this happened in the 9/11 attacks—lack of preparation caused by overconfidence in the leadership will keep them from anticipatory planning and the price can be fatal.

"What you can tolerate you cannot change."—Mike Murdock

The Spiritual Component of Foresight

Even foresight has a spiritual component to it. Preparing for the future is foremost. Forecasting is the ability to make a prediction based on current trends, whereas foresight illustrates insight or knowledge of the future; an understanding of the future from a bird's eye view. Foresight predicts the action of forecasting and what may happen in the future. I will give several biblical scenarios where God gave leaders this insight and as a result they prepared for what was to come.

Noah—Genesis 6: 11-21—God gave Noah foresight that the world would end with rain, so much rain that the earth would be flooded. He foretold Noah that he and his family would be the only ones saved from the flood. In addition to this forecast, he gave Noah the "specs" to build the first ship ever built. In Genesis 7, God goes into detail about who should go into the ark and when they should enter and lock the door.

Abraham—Genesis 12—God gave Abraham foresight to move to a distant land. God forecasted that He would make him into a great nation, make his name great and that He (God) would bless those who blessed him (Abraham) and curse those who cursed him. Then later in Genesis 18, God again forecasts that Abraham and Sarah, both in their 90s, would have a son within that year; this son will confirm making Abraham the father of many nations.

Moses—Exodus 9—God gives Moses insight to go to Pharaoh and tell him to "let my people go, so they can worship Me." God also gives Moses foresight about how it will go—saying that Pharaoh will refuse repeatedly, then let the Hebrews go. It's important to recognize that God's foresight was not that Pharaoh would not merely be reluctant to let the Hebrews go—he would be extremely anxious that they leave, after several progressively worse plagues upon the country of Egypt.

Joseph—In Genesis 37, Joseph had dreams that would be realized. God gave Joseph foresight and Joseph forecasted that one day his eleven brothers would bow down before him. He was given this foresight in his dreams—as a kid he was excited and informed his brothers who became angry and sold him into Egyptian slavery. Genesis 42—many, many years later the brothers came to Egypt in search of food. Without knowing, the brothers bowed down to Joseph—now the second-highest official in Egypt—just as God had forecasted.

Daniel—In this account of forecasts, Daniel 2 tells that he, a young boy, was given the foresight to interpret Nebuchadnezzar's dream about the King's future. In Daniel 5, he received divine foresight again and interpreted the handwriting on the wall meant. Then when Daniel was an elderly man, in Daniel 7-9, he received a series of visions (foresight/forecast) of the very distant future. Many forecasts correlate directly with the visions (forecasts) that John the Apostle received and chronicled in what we now know as the Bible's Book of Revelation.

Jesus—in the books of Matthew, Mark, Luke, and John are repeated accounts of Jesus forecasting the future. He spoke about his mission on earth and about things happening in the next town (before courier mail, email and cell phones). He spoke about his impending future (death) and about the future of the Christian (which at the time were just followers of the Christ). Jesus was future-oriented: He spoke, forecasted, and lived for the future. This gave him direction and people hope for a brighter tomorrow.

The Book of Revelation—from cover to cover, the Book of Revelation is steeped in futurology, with foresights (many which have manifested) and forecasts. This book is centered upon what is to come, and has detailed accounts. But this was the case from the beginning, as depicted in Genesis! God always gave detailed foresight and forecast of exactly what would happen—giving people the opportunity to change that possible future. They rarely took advantage of their power, even knowing what was ahead.

These accounts of historic biblical characters that had amazing foresight to forecast the future were about the pioneers in foresight planning. We look to more recent accounts with men such as Thomas Edison who had foresight and discovered how to harness electricity, this discovery totally changed the world. There are so many reports of what we deem as everyday people who have understood foresight and have impacted the world with their revelations.

There is Alexander Graham Bell, Bill Gates, Steve Jobs and many others. Foresight, forecasting, innovation, and creativity is about having a divine vision—foresight (which is all a God given gift) and forecast a future event or trend (spiritual understanding) and foresight planning—understanding a range of possible futures and use that information to develop a plan (a prerequisite for developing a good, clear strategy).

From the beginning of time, foresight and forecasting were critical to making any plan for the future. God is a huge advocate for the future. He gives insight, foresight, and helps us discover forecasts that will help us achieve a positive future. He said *"For I know the plans I have for you, plans to prosper you and not harm you, plans to give you hope and a great future"*— Jeremiah 29:11.

Any attempt to be successful in business or even in life would be irresponsible without a clear strategic plan. But if you add the spiritual component to any foresight strategic plan, you will see the amazing success these ancient men had. Because they incorporated anticipatory intelligence, they had wealth, left their children large inheritances, and lived long, healthy, and prosperous lives.

Each segment of this book explained the importance of preparation for the shift in leadership for the Latino. Here's what we ascertained—we:

➢ Covered the history of the Latino in America.

➢ Discussed the trends and preparatory management for a positive future.

➢ Explained Emotional Intelligence and the high EQi scores in the Latino population.

➢ Explored CQ and the relevance to this rising global market.

➢ Explained the values, morals and ethics that the Latinos have had ingrained in them so much that assimilating to different value system has been at best—difficult.

➢ Covered the drivers of change and the impact on the Hispanic business leader—we explained how drivers of change have repositioned Latinos.

➢ Examined Foresight Planning and its implication to Latino business.

➢ Discussed Spirituality in Business—here we went through every aspect of business and how connecting spirituality to business is critical for business success.

The jury is in—according to both secular and faith-based schools of thought spirituality belongs in business. Spirituality is at the core of every aspect of our lives, whether you are, or are not, a religious person. Spirituality in business fuses our spirit with our intellect, giving the ability to create wealth (Deuteronomy 8:18). Spirituality fuses while non-spirituality divides and compartmentalizes, making it frustrating for individuals to be whole and operate in wholeness.

There are a few final things which are also essential to business success; attitude of gratitude and being charitable. It is important to maintain an attitude of gratitude. We should always look for the positive in the company, employees, vendors and clientele. Employee recognition is fundamental in any company that wants to prosper. When leaders focus on the positive and the strengths of their staff, making alterations of the weaknesses is easier. Always be grateful always find the positive and your company will be gifted with satisfied employees and customers.

The second is being chartable. I read several years ago about a company in India that gave free lunch to their employees with one request, that employees put money in a jar allocated for a local orphanage. Well, the day came when the leadership decided they would take that money and buy iPods for each child in the orphanage and the employees would get the afternoon off and they would go hand the iPods to children. The results: the following year the employees gave more money and many went out to the community and to friends and family to collect more money in order to give the children more gives. Charity is key! Only givers receive the blessing of always having. I live by the rule that "the giver always has to give while the receiver always has a need." The spiritual law is Be charitable in a variety of ways and your company will prosper.

Finally, what I resolved at the end of my exploration for information is that there is not nearly enough research done on the implications of Latino leadership in the U.S. The concern is that by default, the rapidly rising numbers in the Latino population and their multicultural experiences will cause the Latino to be the largest pool of candidates for leadership roles; but are Latinos ready for this shift? I submit that there is currently a need for training in areas of business, academe, and multiculturalism. There are two tornados brewing: 1) the increase in Latinos in the U.S., and 2) the need for global leaders—the collision is inevitable. Preparation is imperative.

References

Chapter 1

Abalos, D.T. (2007). Latinos in the United States: The Sacred and the Political. Notre Dame, IN: University of Notre Dame Press.

Bedolla, L.G. (2003). Fluid Borders: Latino Power, Identity, and Politics in Los Angeles. Los Angeles: University of California Press.

Bureau of Business Research. The Census Bureau Briefing: Overview of Race and Hispanic Origin: Census 2010. http://www.census.gov/prod/cen2010/briefs/c2010br-02.pdf

Benitez, C., Gonzalez, M. (2011). Latinization and the Latino Leader: How to Value, Develop, and Advance Talented Professionals. Ithaca, NY: Paramount.

Camacho-Liu, M. Investing in Higher Education for Latinos Trends in Latino College Access and Success. http://www.ncsl.org/documents/educ/trendsinlatinosuccess.pdf

Camayd-Freixas, E. (2013). US Immigration Reform and Its Global Impact: Lessons from the Postville Raid. New York, NY. Palgrave-MacMillan.

Cartagena, Chiqui (2013-03-20). Latino Boom II - Catch the Biggest Demographic Wave Since the Baby Boom (Kindle Locations 392-419). Custom Worthy Editions. Kindle Edition.

Chavez, L. (1992). Out of the Barrio: Toward a New Politics of Hispanic Assimilation. New York, NY: Perseus Books Basic Books.

Dávila, A., (2008). The Latino Spin: Public Image and the Whitewashing of Race. New York, NY. New York University Press.

Llagas,C., Snyder, T.D. (2003). Status and Trends in the Education of Hispanics. National Center for Education Statistics: U.S. Department of Education Institute for Education Sciences.

Llopis, G. (2010). The Six Reasons Why Hispanic Leadership will Save America's Corporations. Glenn Llopis Group LLC. (e-book) All Rights Reserved.

Llopis, G. (2011). The Immigrant Perspective on Business Leadership. White Paper: Glenn Llopis Group LLC.

Lopez, M.H. (2009). Latinos in Education: Explaining the Attainment Gap. Retrieved 3/28/12. http://www.pewhispanic.org/2009/10/07/latinos-and-education-explaining-the-attainment-gap/

Neilson, A.C. (2012). *The State of the Hispanic Consumer: The Hispanic Market Imperative.* http://www.nielsen.com/us/en/reports/2012/state-of-the-hispanic-consumer-the-hispanic-market-imperative.html

Nahn, D. (2012). *Buying Power of Hispanics Worth $1Trillion* http://www.nationaljournal.com/thenextamerica/demographics/buying-power-of-hispanics-worth-1-trillion-report-says-20120508

Roach, R. (2013). *Analysis: 2012 Higher Education Enrollment Rate of Latino High School Graduates Surpassed that of Whites.* http://diverseeducation.com/article/55874/#

Chapter 2

Allen, J.C. (2013). Emotional Intelligence Book: Emotional Intelligence at Work and Emotional Intelligence Leadership. Kindle Book.

Bar-On, R. (2006). The Bar-On Model of Emotional-Social Intelligence (ESI). Consortium for Research on Emotional Intelligence in Organizations.

Cook, C.R. (2006). Effects of Emotional Intelligence on Principals' Leadership Performance. Dissertation Bozeman, MO. Montana State University.

Corona, M.A. The Relationship between Emotional Intelligence and Transformational Leadership: A Hispanic American Examination. The Business Journal of Hispanic Research 2010, Vol.4, No. 1 22-34.

Fancher, R.E. (1985) The Intelligence Men: Makes of the IQ Controversy. New York, NY: Norton.

Gardner, L., Stough, C. (2002). "Examining the Relationship between Leadership and Emotional Intelligence in Senior Level Managers." Leadership Organizational. Development Journal, 23(1/2), 68–79.

Goleman, D., Boyatzis, R., & McGee, A. (2002). Primal leadership: Realizing the power of emotional intelligence. Boston, MA: Harvard Business School Press.

Goleman; D. Emotional Intelligence (EQ). BusinessBall.com http://www.businessballs.com/eq.htm

Goleman, D. (1995). Emotional Intelligence. New York: Bantam Books.

Goleman, Daniel (1998). Working With Emotional Intelligence. New York: Bantam Books.

Goleman, D. (2011). Dr. Daniel Goleman on Emotional Intelligence. http://blog.leadertoleader.org/post/Dr-Daniel-Goldman-on-Emotional-Intelligence.aspx

Goleman, D. (1998). What Makes a Leader? Harvard Business Review.

Greenleaf, R. (1977). Servant Leadership: A Journey into the Nature of Legitimate Power & Greatness. Mahwah, NJ., Paulist Press.

Hannay. M, Fretwell, C. Who will be a Servant Leader? Those with High Emotional Intelligence Please Step Forward!

Hofstedes, G. (1991). Cultures and Organizations. Berkshire, England: MacGrawHill.

Jordan, P.J., Troth, A. Emotional Intelligence and Leader Member Exchange: The Relationship with Employee Turnover intentions and Job Satisfaction. Leadership & Organization Development Journal, Vol. 32 No. 3 2011.pp 260-280.

Llopis, 2013 Llopis, G. (2011). The Immigrant Perspective on Business Leadership. White Paper: Glenn Llopis Group LLC.

Leaf, C. (2007). Who Switched Off My Brain: Controlling Toxic Thoughts and Emotions. Dallas, TX. Switch on Brain Ltd.

Livermore, D. (2010). Leading with Cultural Intelligence. New York, NY.

Lugo, M. Cultural and Emotional Intelligences in the Development of Global Transformational Leadership Skills. Bridgewater College, Bridgewater, VA.

Mayer,J.D., Salovey, P., Carusso, D. Emotional Intelligence: Theory, Findings and Implications. Psychological Inquiry 2004, Vol. 15, No. 3, 197-215

Melchar, D.E. & Bosco, S.M. (2010). Achieving High Organization Performance through Servant Leadership.

Ramirez, A.R 2006. Impact of Cultural Intelligence Level on Conflict Resolution Ability: A Conceptual Model and Research Proposal. Emerging Leadership Journeys, Vol.3 Iss. 1 2010. Pp. 45-56.

Reilly, A.H., Karounos, T.J. Exploring the Link between Emotional Intelligence and Cross Cultural Leadership Effectiveness. Journal of International Business and Cultural Studies.

Vance, C., & Paik, Y. (2006). Global workforce training and development. Managing a global workforce: Challenges and Opportunities in International Human Resource Management. New York, NY: Sharpe Publications.

Winston, B. (1999). Be a Manager for God's Sake: Essays about the Perfect Manager. Virginia Beach, VA: Regent University School of Business.

Winston, B. E., & Hartsfield, M. (2004). Similarities between Emotional Intelligence and Servant Leadership. http://www.regent.edu/acad/cls/2004SLRoundtable/winston-2004SL.pdf

Chapter 3

Abalos, D.T. (2007). Latinos in the United States: The Sacred and the Political. Notre Dame, IN: University of Notre Dame Press.

Benitez, C., Gonzalez, M. (2011). Latinization and the Latino Leader: How to Value, Develop, and Advance Talented Professionals. Ithaca, NY: Paramount Market Publishing, Inc.

Bordas, J. (2013). The Power of Latino Leadership: Culture, Inclusion and Contribution. San Francisco, CA: Berrett-Koehler Publishers, Inc.

Covey, S. (2005). The 8th Habit: From Effectiveness to Greatness. New York: NY: FreePress.

Ciulla, J. (2004). Ethics, the Heart of Leadership. Westport, Connecticut: Praeger.

Erickson, H. (2009). Excerpts from Before You Go: Preparation for Short Term Mission. http://aguavivahome.org/userfiles/files/hispanic%20culture%20values.pdf

Gousmett, C. (1996). Introduction to a Christian worldview: A Course in Thinking Christianly About the Whole of Life. http://www.allofliferedeemed.co.uk/Gousmett/CGWorldviewManual.pdf

Hall, E.T. (1973). The Silent Language. New York, NY: Anchor Books

Hall, L. (1998). No Longer I. Abilene, TX: ACU Press.

Hofstede, G. (2001). Culture's Consequences: Comparing Values, Behaviors, Institutions, and Organizations Across Nations. Sage Publications.

Hofstede, G. & Hofstede, G.J. (2005). Cultures and Organizations Software of the Mind: Intercultural Cooperation and Its Importance for Survival. New York, NY: McGraw-Hill.

Joas, H. (2000). The genesis of values. Chicago: University of Chicago.

Katz, L. (2006). Negotiating International Business: The Negotiators Reference Guide to 50 Countries Around the World. BookSurge.com.

Kohls, L.R. The Values Americans Live By
http://www.claremontmckenna.edu/pages/faculty/alee/extra/Am erican_values.html

Kotter, J. P. (1999). Leading Change. Boston: Harvard Business Review Press.

Lopez-Baez,S .(1999). Marianismo. In J.S. Mio, J.E. Trimble, P. Arredondo, H.E. Cheatham, & D. Sue (Eds.). Westport, CT: Greenwood Press

Loretta Marketing Group. Core Values and General Cultural Insights of U.S. Hispanics. http://www.slideshare.net/JimLoretta/core-values-and-general-cultural-insights-of-us-hispanics-4133624

Llopis,G. (2013). The Six Reasons Why Hispanic Leadership Will Save American's Corporations. E-book.

Llopis, G. (2011). The Immigrant Perspective on Business Leadership. White Paper: Glenn Llopis Group LLC.

Marin, G., & Triandis, H.C. 1985. Allocentrism as an Important Characteristic of the Behavior of Latin Americans and Hispanics. Cross-Cultural and National Studies of Social Psychology (pp. 85-114). Amsterdam: North Holland.

Markus, H.R.,   Kitayama, S. (1991). Culture and the Self: Implication for Cognition, Emotion and Motivation. Psychological Review 1991, Vol. 98, No. 2, pp 224-253

Malphurs, A. (2004). Values Driven Leadership: Discovering and Developing Your Core Values for Ministry. Grand Rapids, MI: Baker Books.

Marcum, D., Smith, S. (2007). Egonomics: what makes ego our greatest asset (or most expensive liability). New York, NY: Fireside.

Oyerman, D., Lee, S.W.S. Does Culture Influence What and How We Think? Effects of Priming Individualism and Collectivism. Psychological Bulletin 2008. American Psychological Association 2008, Vol. 134, No. 2, 311–342

Pajewski, A., & Enriquez, L. (1996). Teaching from a Hispanic perspective: A handbook for non-Hispanic adult educators. Phoenix, AZ: Arizona Adult Literacy and Technology Resource Center.

Rodriguez, R. (2008). Latino Talent: Effective Strategies to Recruit, Retain, and Develop Hispanic Professionals. Hoboken, NJ. Wiley& Sons Inc.

Santiago-Rivera, A. L., Arredondo, P., & Gallardo-Cooper, M. (2002). Counseling Latinos and la familia: A practical guide. Thousand Oaks, CA:Sage Publications.

Szapocznik, J., Kurtines, W. M., & Fernandez, T. (1980). Bicultural involvement and adjustment in Hispanic American youths. International Journal of Intercultural Relations, 4, 353-366.

Szapocznik, J., Kurtines, W. M., Foote, E., Pérez-Vidal, A., & Hervis, O. E. (1986). Conjoint versus one-person family therapy: Further evidence for the effectiveness of conducting family therapy through one person. Journal of Consulting and Clinical Psychology, 54, 395-397.

Smokowski, P. R., Rose, R., & Bacallao, M. L. (2008). Acculturation and Latino family processes: How cultural involvement, biculturalism, and acculturation gaps influence family dynamics. Family Relations, 57(3), 295-308.

Sweeny, M. 2011. Regent University DSL candidate. Values in an Organization (dialogue).

Winston, B. E. (2006). Leadership style as an outcome of motive: A contingency 'state' rather than 'trait' concept. Unpublished manuscript, Regent University, Virginia Beach, VA.

Young, M. (2011). Characteristics and Needed Assistance of Hispanic Women Business Owners: Emerging Entrepreneurs. Small Business Institute Journal No. 7 April, 2011.

Zimbardo, P.G., Boyd, J.N. Putting Time into Perspective: A Valid, Reliable Individual-Differences Metric. Journal of Personality and Social Psychology, 1999, Vol., 77, No. 6, 1271-1288.

Chapter 4

Abalos, D.T. (2007). Latinos in the United States: The Sacred and the Political. Notre Dame, IN: University of Notre Dame Press.

Agilera,E. (2013). Latino College Graduates: Don't Stop Now. http://www.huffingtonpost.com/esther-aguilera/latino-college-graduates_b_3398265.html

Bishop, P. & Hines, A. (2012). Social change. In Teaching about the future. New York, NY; Palgrace Macmillian.

Blaine, B. (2000). The psychology of diversity: Perceiving and experiencing social difference. Mountain View, CA: Mayfield.

Briggs, Bush Center, (2013). The Education of Immigrants. http://www.bushcenter.org/blog/2013/07/10/education-immigrants

Cartagena, C. (2005). Latino Boom! Everything You Need to Know to Grow Your Business in the U.S. Hispanic Market. New York, NY: Random House Inc.

Cartagena, Chiqui (2013-03-20). Latino Boom II - Catch the Biggest Demographic Wave Since the Baby Boom (Kindle Locations 392-419). Custom Worthy Editions. Kindle Edition.

Cárdenas, V., Kerby, S. (2012). The State of Latinos in the United States Although This Growing Population Has Experienced Marked Success, Barriers Remain http://www.americanprogress.org/issues/race/report/2012/08/08/11984/the-state-of-latinos-in-the-united-states/

Chavez, L. (1992). Out of the Barrio: Toward a New Politics of Hispanic Assimilation. New York, NY: Perseus Books Basic Books.

Corrigan, P. (2004). How stigma interferes with mental health care. American Psychologist, 59, 614 – 625.

Chavez, L. (1992). Out of the Barrio: Toward a New Politics of Hispanic Assimilation. New York, NY: Perseus Books Basic Books.

Dávila, A., (2008). The Latino Spin: Public Image and the Whitewashing of Race. New York, NY. New York University Press.

Chapa, J. (2002). "Affirmative Action, X Percent Plans, and Latino Access to Higher Education in the Twenty-first Century." In Latinos:The Remaking of America by Marcelo M. Suarez-Orozco and Mariela Paez. Berkley, CA. University of California Press.

Gonzalez, J. (2000). A History of Latinos in America: Harvest of Empire. London, England: Penguin Books.

Gomez, E. (2011). Latino-Owned Businesses: Leading the Recovery. Pew Research Hispanic Trends. http://www.forbes.com/sites/evangelinegomez/2011/12/28/latino-owned-businesses-leading-the-recovery/

Koebler, J. (2011). Growing Hispanic Population Is Spreading Across U.S. The nation's Hispanic population reaches 50 million

U.S. News, http://www.usnews.com/news/articles/2011/03/25/growing-hispanic-population-is-spreading-across-us

Llopis, 2013 Llopis, G. (2011). The Immigrant Perspective on Business Leadership. White Paper: Glenn Llopis Group LLC.

Lopez, M.H. & Motel, S. (2012). Latinos Express Growing Confidence in Personal Finances, Nation's Direction. http://www.pewhispanic.org/2012/11/02/latinos-express-growing-confidence-in-personal-finances-nations-direction/

Orchowski, P. (2011). Don't Assume the Hispanic Vote Is a Democratic Lock Latinos are the most diverse 'ethnic' group in the country. USNews.com.

http://www.usnews.com/opinion/articles/2011/08/05/dont-assume-the-hispanic-vote-is-a-democratic-lock

Pew Research: Social & Demographic Trends http://www.pewsocialtrends.org/

Pew Hispanic Center. Wealth gap widens between whites and Hispanics. Washington, DC: Author; October 18, 2004. (Wealth report).

McClellan, S. (2013). Upscale Hispanics Increase Size, Spending Power Santiago Solutions Group http://santiagosolutionsgroup.com/upscale-hispanics-increase-size-spending-power-media-daily-news/

Reimers C., Hispanics and the future of America. National Research Council Washington, DC: Panel on Hispanics in the United States, Committee on Population, Division of Behavioral and Social Sciences and Education, The National Academies Press; 2006. Economic well-being. (Ch. 8)

U.S. Census Bureau - http://www.census.gov/

U.S. Census 2010 - http://www.census.gov/2010census/

Vago, S. (2004). Social Change. Saddle River, NJ: Pearson-Prentice Hall.

Vallejo, A. (2012). Latina Spaces: Middle-Class Ethnic Capital and Professional Associations in the Latino Community. Department of Sociology, University of Southern California. American Sociological Association.

Vogel, D.L., Bitman, R.L., Hammer, J.H., Wade, N.G. (2013). Is Stigma Internalized? The Longitudinal Impact of Public Stigma on Self-Stigma. Journal of Counseling and Psychology, 2013 April; Vol. 60 (2):311-6

Yen, H. (2012). Census: White Population Will Lose Majority In U.S. By 2043. Latino Politics, http://www.huffingtonpost.com/2012/12/12/census-hispanics-and-black-unseat-whites-as-majority-in-united-states-population_n_2286105.html

Chapter 5

Ashley, W. C., Morrison, J. L. (1995). Anticipatory Management: 10 power tools for excellence into the 21st century. Leesburg, VA: Issue Action.

BusinessDictionary.com.
http://www.businessdictionary.com/definition/foresight.html

Courtney, H., Kirkland, J., & Viguerie, P. (Nov-Dec 1997). "Strategy under uncertainty (business forecasting)". Harvard Business Review 75.n6: pp66 (14).

Copulsky, et al. (2013). Adapt. Evolve. Transform. Business Trends 2013. Deloitte University Press.

Durante, N. (2011). Nancy Durante Talks TedX East.
http://www.youtube.com/watch?v=UfQF3DXG-S4

Gordon, T.J. Interactive Scenarios. World Future Society.

Gordon, T.J., Glenn, J.C. Environmental Scanning. World Future Society.

Bishop, P., and Hines A. (2006). Thinking about the future: Guidelines for strategic foresight. Washington, DC: Social Technologies, LCC.

Investopedia
http://www.investopedia.com/terms/s/strategicalliance.asp#ixzz2M1SQV000

Jannek, K., Burmeister, K. (2007). Corporate Foresight in Small and Medium-Sized Enterprises. The Foresight Company. Foresight Brief No. 101

McGonigal, J. (2011). Reality Broken: Why Games Make Us Better and How They Can Change the World. Strand, London:Penguin Books.

Molitor, Graham T. (2003). Molitor Forecasting Model: Key Dimensions for Plotting the "Patterns of Change" Journal of Future Studies, August 2003, 8(1): pgs. 61-72.

Molitor, G. T. (2003). The power to change the world: The art of forecasting. Potomac, MD: Public Policy Forecasting.

Mintzberg, H., Ahlstrand, B. & Lampel, J. (1998). Strategy Safari: A guided tour through the wilds of strategic management. New York: Free Press.

Pfohl, R.M. (2012). Moving from Strategic Planning to Streategic Resilience through Anticipatory Management Practices. United Health Group.

Wilson, I., Ralston, B. (2006). The scenario-planning handbook: A practitioner's guide to developing and using scenarios to direct strategy in today's uncertain times. Mason, OH: South-Western Educational.

Vago, S. (2004). Social Change. Saddle River, NJ: Pearson-Prentice Hall.

Van der Heijden, K.V. (2005). Scenarios: The Art of Strategic Conversation. West Sussex, ENG./John Wiley & Sons

World Future Society (2004).

Chapter 6

Aburdene, P. (2005). Megatrends 2010: The rise of Conscious Capitalism. Charlottesville, VA: Library of Congress.

Flax, B. (2011). The True Meaning of Separation of Church and State. Forbes.com
http://www.forbes.com/sites/billflax/2011/07/09/the-true-meaning-of-separation-of-church-and-state/

Giblin, J.C. (2002). The Life and Death of Adolf Hitler. New York, NY: Clarion Books.

Greenleaf, R. (1977). Servant Leadership: A Journey into the Nature of Legitimate Power & Greatness. Mahwah, NJ. Paulist Press.

Greenleaf,R.K. (1970) What is Servant Leadership. Retrieved 11/9/10 http://www.greenleaf.org/whatissl/

Hannay. M, Fretwell, C. Who will be a Servant Leader? Those with High Emotional Intelligence Please Step Forward!

Hughes, B.B.; Hillerbrand, E.E. (2006). Exploring and Shaping International Futures. Boulder, CO: Paradigm Publishers

Holy Bible (2000). Life Application Study Bible– New American Standard Bible. La Habra, CA:

Malphurs, A. (2004). Values Driven Leadership: Discovering and Developing Your Core Values for Ministry. Grand Rapids, MI: Baker Books.

Marques, J., Dhiman, S., King, R. (2007). *Spirituality in the Workplace: What It Is, Why It Matters, How to Make It Work for You.* Fawnskin, CA.: Personhood Press.

Maxwell, J. (2003). Developing Leaders Around You: How to Help Other Reach Their Full Potential, Nashville, TN.: Injoy, Inc.

McLaughlin,C. The Fourth Dimension Inc.: Towards Integral Management. Sri Aurobindo Society - http://fdi.sasociety.in/cms/index.php/fdi/article/95_Spirituality_an d_Ethics_in_Business

McLaughlin, C. (2009). Spirituality and Ethics in Business. http://www.visionarylead.org/articles/spbus.htm

Mitroff, I.I., Denton, E.A. (1999). A Spiritual Audit of Corporate America: Ten Years Later Spirituality and Attachment Therory, an Interim Report http://ccrm.berkeley.edu/pdfs_papers/2.09/New_Spirituality_Pap erfinal(2).pdf

Nkwasibwe, F.L. (2012). Business Courage: Integrating Spirituality and Culture at the Workplace. Mustange, OK: Tate Publishing & Enterprises, LLC.

O'Toole, J. (1996). Leading change: The argument for values-based leadership. San Francisco: Jossey-Bass.

Peacocke, D. "Empowering People in and for Marketplace Ministry" November/December 2002 edition of Business Reform Magazine. http://www.intheworkplace.com/apps/articles/default.asp?rticleid=55441&columnid=1935

Toland, J. (1976). Adolf Hitler. Garden City, NY: Anchor Books.

Walker, M. (2005). A Comparison Study of Protestants in the Workplace; What Effect does a Church Workplace Ministry have on Protestant Workers' Job Satisfaction, Organizational Citizenship Behavior, and Organizational Commitment within Certain Faith Integration Types? Dissertation at Regent University School of Leadership Studies for PhD.

WebMD.com. Managing Job Stress. http://www.webmd.com/balance/stress-management/managing-job-stress

Winston, B. E. (2006). Leadership style as an outcome of motive: A contingency 'state' rather than 'trait' concept. Unpublished manuscript, Regent University, Virginia Beach, VA.

Nasser, H.E., (2010). U.S. Hispanics Outliving Whites and Blacks. USA Today
http://www.usatoday.com/news/health/2010-10-13-hispanics-life-span_N.htm

National Council of La Raza (NCLR). 20 FAQS About Hispanics.
http://www.nclr.org/index.php/about_us/faqs/most_frequently_asked_questions_about_hispanics_in_the_us/

Orozco-Suarez, M.M., Páez, M.M. (2002). Latino's Remaking America. London, England. University of California Press

National Research Council.
http://www.nationalacademies.org/nrc/

Minority Business Development Agency.
http://www.commerce.gov/os/ogc/minority-business-development-agency

Pew Hispanic Center National Survey. Social and Demographic Trends. http://www.pewsocialtrends.org/

Rodriguez, R. (2008). Latino Talent: Effective Strategies to Recruit, Retain, and Develop Hispanic Professionals. Hoboken, NJ. Wiley& Sons Inc.

Tienda, M., Mitchell, F. (2006). Hispanics and the Future of America. Washington, D.C. The National Research Council.

The Hispanic Institute. The Hispanic Institute of Columbia University. Department of Latin American Studies and Cultures http://www.columbia.edu/cu/spanish/hispanicinstitute/hispinstintro.html

The Julian Somora Research Institute. http://msutoday.msu.edu/news/2010/julian-samora-research-institute-identifies-top-issues-facing-michigan-latinos/

U.S. Census Bureau. The Census Bureau Briefing: Overview of Race and Hispanic Origin: Census 2010. http://www.census.gov/prod/cen2010/briefs/c2010br-02.pdf

ABOUT THE AUTHOR

Nilda Perez holds a doctorate in Strategic Leadership, focused on Global Business and Strategic Foresight from the school of Business and Leadership, Regent University, Virginia Beach, VA., in 2013.

Nilda is a published author, keynote speaker, consultant, and coach. She has specialized in business training and workshops that focus on creating and enhancing business. She trains using a series of modules, all of which are geared towards leadership, core values and ethics, emotional intelligence, creative mindset, drivers of change, strategic foresight, and spirituality in the workplace. She also does training on successful business start-ups that will sustain these uncertain times.

She is also the Founder of the Aspire 4 Life Inc™, and The Latino Academy for Business™. Both focus on 21st Century business development. Her background in psychology, social theory, systems theory, future studies, business, and in-depth passion for research create a unique from which she offers uncommon perspectives for massive change.

The Latino Academy for Business™ is equipped to thoroughly train businesses with cutting-edge strategies for growth and sustainability. The highly qualified staff whose goals are to help you achieve your business goals. Through education we build any size business and assist in elevating the leadership of staff to achieve their highest performance. A4B creates a partnership with business so together we can create solutions that are often difficult for businesses to achieve individually. We offer a series of training sessions and workshops which concentrate on bringing businesses through the 21st century successfully.

We are proficient in both English and Spanish and offer every consultation, coaching, training, and workshop in English, Spanish and bi-lingual (both languages simultaneously) formats. This helps the growing number of Latino businesses to take advantage of these trainings in their native language. Our goal is to help you achieve your business goals with techniques that are current, relevant and have the ability to catapult your business to unprecedented levels.

Dr. Nilda Perez, DSL, LCSW-R, CCLC
Speaker, Consultant and Coach
The Latino Academy for Business™
Aspire 4 Life Inc.
Consulting, Training and Coaching Services
http://www.LatinoAcademyforBusiness.com
Off Ph: 845-206-4602
Fax: 866-494-9697
Skype: nilda-perez

www.ingramcontent.com/pod-product-compliance
Lightning Source LLC
Chambersburg PA
CBHW071548200326
41519CB00021BB/6647